The Broadaway Slave Journey

MARIE TOMS

ISBN: 9798328617116

DEDICATION

The dedication of this book is to our ancestors who found the positive in all situations:

- A Slave whether born a slave or brought over from Africa.
- A Slave sold to the highest bidder in their lifetime.
- A Slave allowed to attend church for the good of the slave master.
- A Slave but found a way to learn how to read and write.
- A Slave who bore children for their Masters/Owners.
- A Slave that shared their inferred spouses with the slave masters.
- A Slave that worked as laborers, field hands, housekeepers, and cooks.
- A Slave community of God-fearing people.
- A former Slave fought in the Confederate army for $12.00 a month.
- A former Slave who taught others how to read and write. (It was against the law)
- A former Slave who practiced "Yes, Boss."
- A former Slave who struggled to give an opinion and to show your "Smarts."
- A former Slave Inventor.
- A former Slave Minister.
- A former Slave Community and Individuals that secured some of their culture.
- A Former Slaves and Colored people who started Black townships.
- A Former Slaves who created another way to survive, once freed.
- A Freed Slave Ancestors who paved the way for us.
- A Freed men and women who taught us that we are not less than.
- An African Americans who struggled through Jim Crow laws, like guessing the number of shelled peas in a gallon jar before voting. If you guessed incorrectly, you didn't get to vote.
- An African Americans who struggled through inequality in education denied grants and education funding.
- An African Americans who dealt with inequality and segregation.
- An African Americans who deal with inequality and integration.
- An African Americans who dealt with inequality in work and pay.

Our ancestors struggled through so much. As descendants our path may not be clear, but we believe that our struggle can produce successes. We must follow the strength and fiber of our ancestors. We look forward to the future. We claim success.

HOW TO USE THIS BOOK

For easy reading, we divided this book Broadaway Slave Journey into seven main family branches grouped by the patriarch's name. You may locate your family at the top of the tree or wherever you see your great-grand or grandparents' name. Remember this is just a start. Here's to discovering more about your Broadaway family.

Marie Broadway Toms

CONTENTS

ACKNOWLEDGMENTS

We acknowledge anyone who helped in the process of research or life in general to make this project a successful one.

Thank God for guiding us through the paths and allowing the Broadways to share our ancestral history through the publishing of ten Broadway books. *Eugene Broadway* is the Broadway and Broadaway family's number one researcher. He has maintained our Broadway ancestry tree and researched every day for fourteen years. With Eugene's work the Broadway family tree has grown to over 39,000 relatives in the ancestry database.

Hassan Broadway, Jerome Turner, and *Marie Broadway Toms* are all responsible for a tremendous amount of research and work. *Hassan Broadway* authored the very first detailed booklet about the Broadway family's migration from North Carolina. *Marie Toms* has authored four family history books including two Broadway books, two Peppers books, coordinated the publishing process for Jerome and Eugene's books and one Toms book. *Jerome Turner* has authored two family history books and *Eugene Broadway* has authored three family history books.

In the previous books, family stories were written. Every branch of the Broadway/Broadaway tree has contributed to the research of family trees with family names, birthdates, death dates, residences, stories and hints about the family, photographs, obituaries, interviews, cemetery inventories, et cetera.

Thanks to everyone. Thanks to our publisher, Earma Brown, for ten years of support. Without her, we may not have published any books.

THE BROADAWAY SLAVE JOURNEY FAQ

1.   **Why are there Broadaway and Broadway surnames from the same family?**

Answer: For example, Marshall Baucom Broadaway and Marshall C. Broadaway were looking for a new start in Arkansas. They may have changed the surname for that reason. Research documents verify the surname changed in 1900.

Broadway family historians agree, White Census workers may have misspelled the surname when pronounced Broadaway and our ancestors didn't make a fuss. It was a small group of Black Broadaways who came to the 'Land of Opportunity' from North Carolina in the late 1880s. Additionally, it was never quite confirmed since most of the 1890 US Federal Census records were destroyed in a fire in Washington, D.C..

2.   **Why did Marshall Baucom Broadaway change his surname to Broadway?**

 Answer: Marshall Baucom's father is listed as "James Broadaway" on Marshall and Silvey Broadaway's marriage certificate in 1873. He took the opportunity to drop the last slave owner's name, Baucom, and used his previous slave owner's name, Broadaway. Also, he wanted to use the same name as his father.

3.   **Who are the researchers for Broadway/Broadaway family research?**

Answer: Every family had volunteers to gather family history. Some families compiled information in the form of an obituary collection, spreadsheets, databases, booklets, web sites, books, Ancestry.com and more. The James Broadaway and Marshall B. Broadway descendants have done all the ways listed above. Major contributors in family research are Ken Broadway, Marie Toms, Jerome Turner, and Eugene Broadway.

4.   **Who subscribes to Ancestry.com to keep the large Broadway Family Tree active and ongoing?**

 Answer: Eugene Broadway has maintained and generated research results on Ancestry.com daily since 2009.

5.   **Why is Broadway used within most of the charts on Ancestry.com-Eugene Broadway Subscribed/Managed Tree?**

Answer: Broadway is used within most of the charts to produce hints, findings, and relatives for the Broadway Family trees, then Broadaway trees.

6.   What is the main source of the data presented in this document?

Answer: The main source has been Ancestry.com research generated from 1870-1950 US Federal Census, Slave Schedules, Birth, Marriage, and Death records. Other Ancestry family trees, WWI & WWII draft cards, US SS applications and claims, and land records have been researched. Also, personal interviews, obituaries, church documents, and cemeteries are major sources of research. Furthermore, books, news reports, directories have enabled us to follow hints from previous research, etc.

7.   Why aren't all families and their descendants found in the family trees listed in this book?

Answer: Our family relatives' ancestors' and descendants' trees are massive. Eugene has a tree of 39,000 Broadway relatives which is still expanding. Also, we are trying to give you a start for your own research by giving you all the major ancestors that our current Broadway and Broadaway researchers have found.

8.   Why are Slave owners/masters listed in this book of family history?

Answer: Our commitment threaded throughout the Broadway books has been to excellence, honor, and respect of the families in recording history. Fact finding with trackable sources and telling family stories to inspire the next generation. Furthermore, the author, family historians and researchers thought it would be interesting to most to know about our ancestors' owners as slaves. Some of the family lines came directly from within the Slave owner's household. For example, William Cannie Broadaway is a direct descendant of ancestor and slave owner John Broadaway. There are other interesting connections inside the book.

BROADAWAY FEATURED
PATRIARCHS & MATRIARCHS

In the years 1775-1776 The American Revolution was an insurrection by Patriots in the 13 colonies against British rule, resulting in American independence. Born in 1775, Plantation Owner Jesse Broadaway later owned some of Broadway Family's earliest known ancestors.

Welcome to the Broadaway Slave Journey edition of the Broadway books. This book is a companion to The Broadway Generations, The Journey, Broadway Connections, Broadway Royals and Discovering Your African Culture. Thank you for taking the journey with us through the history pages of the Broadway and Broadaway branches of the family. It was written to introduce the branches of family to each other and provide a foundational way to encourage more research, as far as we can go into our shared ancestry.

Believe it or not, there's still more facts to be discovered and more stories to tell about the Broadway/Broadaway families. With the amount of research already done, our young and young-at-heart need only use their imagination to create wonderful stories that will transport us back to 17th through 19th century times and the lives of our ancestors.

For some of us who have been researching for years, we have developed the trees from earliest known ancestor *James Broadway*, a slave as a young man in the late 1700s to our current newborns and children. We saw his name (James) on one of the slave schedules listed as property of Broadaway slave owners along with other family members including Marshall Broadway at six, as a young slave boy.

We followed them, *James,* and *Marshall,* through research all-the-way through being freed in United States to co-pioneering their own wagon train along with Marshall C. Broadaway, and their families to gain a fresh start in Arkansas, the Land of Opportunity.

After U.S. Emancipation Patriarch James lived out his days in North Carolina, living with his son Marshall and then a relative believed to be his daughter after the Broadway Wagon Train participants left.

From a census report, we discovered Marshall in a small town working on the railroad where he met and married Matriarch Sylvia. Marshall eventually became one of the main pioneers of the family who led the famous wagon train that migrated from the Broadway branch to the Land of Opportunity. (Wagon pictured on cover of first book – painting by Danny Broadway, Memphis Artist).

Our trips, interviews, cemetery visits, fact gathering, research through hundreds of records, obituaries and more made the journey interesting but a lot of work. We encourage you to continue with us in this companion book *The Broadaway Slave Journey*. Hopefully, it will inspire you to do further research into your family branch or entertain us with your works of fiction. Encourage the historians or storytellers in your family and see what happens.

STORY: Our Journey to the Land of Opportunity
Written for Slyvia Broadway (fictional based on true events)

We arrived in a caravan of wagons. It was a sight to see as Massa used to say. I stepped on the freshly rained on brown ground called God's earth. I don't want to make it seem like more than what it was. But everything looked so green, really green and fresh. Maybe it was more of us than what we saw and felt. It seemed as rich as they said. The land of opportunity is what Marsha said the note called it. After we saw the note and decided we should go for it, it was a long year of preparing and planning to make the trip.

At times we didn't know if we would make it—get to travel. Not to mention the rivers, back roads and no roads we traveled. But here we stand, our first day in this land of opportunity. We all made it. There's me--Slyvia and my husband Marsha. Our little ones: John, Oliver, Mary, Anie, William Cannie, Julia, Morris, Julius and Senior Broadway. Daddy James decided not to come. Which was a surprise to all of us. He and Marsha were so close. We did not even think about him not going with us. I had someone write this for us. I wanted to make a record of what happened. It's a big deal among us. A Colored man, a former Slave owning land 133 acres of it too, selling it and moving away.

Not a minute too soon. That green, black monster got so stirred up at times. I figure the green part is the jealousy people have and the black part is the hateful prejudice side. Either side or both sides wants Colored people to NOT get up from slavery. But me and Marsha we prayed and got the ok from God. Massa Broadaway was spiritual, and he taught us spiritual on how to do certain big things. He said look for three okays. He (God) will show you in different ways.

Most of us didn't know how we were going to do for ourselves after Lincoln signed. We listened to that man George Washington Carver on how to grow for ourselves on the side. So, Marsha was in Persons with Sandy Clark and saw the note posted. He asked the store clerk in White Store could he get it, thinking Oliva could read it to us at home. That's our second oldest. He sat with Massa them youngest, David, and learned to read and write. It had to be a secret though.

Back then and even now, not only was it against the law for a Colored to do that. But people would get really mad about it.

Our eyes got really big when Oliva read it and said it's about land for sale. It said, 'Come and buy in the 'Land of Opportunity.' Which was a long way west, though not all the way west. It was unsettled land but the State was back in the Union.

It all started with me meeting Marsha. My mother and I moved to Carolinas with our tribe. We travelled along the Trail of Tears. So, I told Marsha once in a lifetime was enough. The other families agreed They didn't want to go on no trail of tears either. We knew we had to plan carefully.

After we got to North Carolina, we ended up settling in a railroad town called Persons. We worked as maids in the town. We cleaned several of the boarding houses in town for the North Carolina Railways. It was two families and others on our wagon train. We were all so excited we didn't know what to do with ourselves. Like I said earlier, here we are ready for the NEW.

Family Tree Descendants Included in this book:

Broadaway Family History Trivia: According to undocumented sources_Broadaway Slave ancestors may have originated from the slave plantations below: Grandparents of Jesse Broadaway
- John Broadaway 1755-1841 & Sarah Leah Morris 1750-1846
- Rev. S.V. Broadaway 1730-1780 & Elizabeth Denton 1730-1820
- Joseph Barrett 1732-1801 & Mary Ann Sarratt 1735-1798

Section III Jesse Broadaway 1775-1841, Person Co., NC (Slave Master)
1. William "Buck" Broadaway 1804-1877, White Store, Anson & Marshville, Union, NC (Creasie Broadaway 1827) (Slave Master)
2. King Broadaway 1844-1930 Lanesboro & Marshville, Anson, NC
3. John David King Broadaway 1883-1948, Lanesboro & Marshville, Anson, NC
4. Joe Broadaway 1917-1993, Union & Rockingham, NC
5. Joe Fred Broadaway, Lanesboro, Anson, NC
6. Tammy J. Broadaway, Lanesboro, Anson, NC

Section IV Jesse Broadaway 1775-1841, Person Co., NC (Slave Master)
1. William "Buck" Broadaway 1804-1877 (Slave Master) & Creasie Broadaway 1827
2. Creasie Broadaway 1827 Meltonsville & White Store Township, Anson, NC (John Barrett)
3. Marshall C. Broadaway 1847 (Elizabeth-Bettie) Lilesville & Lanesboro, Anson, NC
4. Orlander L. Broadaway 1884-1949 (Broadway), North Carolina, Hampton & Moro, AR

5. Elbert Buster Broadaway 1911-2000, Hampton & Moro, AR
6. Lenora Broadway Wilder, Moro, AR, Chicago, IL

Section V Siblings Broadaway 1795-1850
1. James A Baucom-Broadway 1815–1881
2. Harry Broadway 1815–1887
3. Robert "Bob" Broadway 1817–1881
4. Creasie "Harriett" Broadway 1827–
5. George Broadway 1835–

Section VI Harry Broadaway 1815-1887 Ansonville, Anson, NC
1. Hamilton Broadaway 1841-1880, Anson, NC; North, Orangeburg, South Carolina
2. Lewis Walter Broadaway 1863-1950, Burnsville, Anson, NC 1870-1950
3. Gaston Broadaway 1887-1924, Burnsville, Anson, NC 1900-1920/Clayton Broadaway Sr. 1904-1986, Burnsville, Anson, NC 1910-1950, Polkton, Anson, NC, Albemarle, Stanly, North Carolina 1986
4. Kenneth C. Broadaway 1919-1985, Oakboro, Stanley, NC, Salisbury, Rowan, NC
5. Roderick Craig Broadaway

Section VII James Broadaway 1815-1881, Burnsville & Lanesboro, NC
1. Marshall Baucom-Broadaway1850-1926 (1910 name spelled Broadway) 1850-1926, 1860 Lilesville, 1870 Burnsville, 1880 Lanesboro, NC, 1900 Hampton, Lee, AR (Broadaway), 1910 Hampton, Lee, AR (Broadway), 1920 Hampton, AR, age 65 (Broadway); Flint, MI, 1926 Chicago, Cook, IL
2. Oliver Broadaway (Broadway) 1874-1950, Lanesboro, Anson, NC, Hampton & Moro, AR
3. Samuel Broadway 1901-1992, Hampton & Moro, AR, Chicago, IL
4. Daniel Broadway 1920-1999, Helena, Phillips, AR, Hampton, Lee, AR, Little Rock, AR, Michigan 1951 & Illinois
5. Eugene Broadway, Moro & Little Rock, AR, Atlanta, GA

Section VIII Robert "Bob" Broadaway 1817- (63), Ansonville, Anson, NC
Spouse: Harriet Miney Broadway
1. George "Johnnie" Broadway 1842–1895
2. Lydia Broadway 1849–
3. Harriett Broadway 1855–

Section IX Harriett Broadaway 1805 (75) Wife, married 1853 Union, NC & 1866

1. Lydia Broadaway 1849 (31)
2. Ellen Broadaway 1866 (14) granddaughter
3. Harriett Broadaway 1855 (25)

Section X George Broadaway 1835- Lanesboro Township, Anson, NC

Wives: Phylis Parker 1840- ; Harriet Broadaway 1848-1923 (32)

1. George W Maske 1859-1928
2. Jenia Broadaway 1868
3. Bose Broadaway, 1871
4. James E Broadaway 1874-1940
5. Dave Broadaway, 1878-1914
6. Watt Broadaway 1878
7. Charlotte C. Broadaway 1879

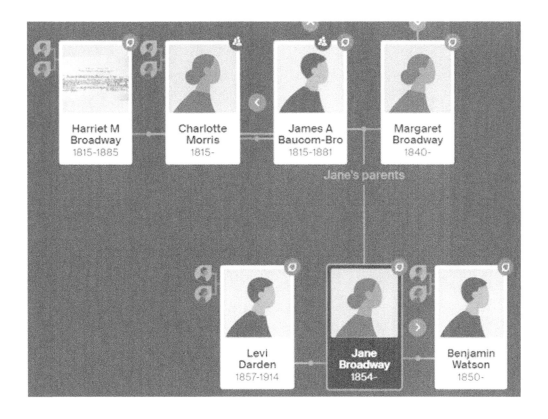

SECTION III THE SLAVE MASTERS

Broadaway Family History Trivia: In 1815 Ancestor James Broadaway was born. Life for the average person in the 1800's was hard. Many lived a hand-to-mouth existence, working long hours in often harsh conditions. There was no electricity, running water or central heating.

Slave Masters (SM) Jesse Broadaway 1775-1841 and William "Buck" Broadaway 1804-1877 Featured in Section III and IV are introduced with one branch of slave ancestors and descendants.

Jesse Broadaway (SM) 1775-1841

Jesse Broadaway was born in 1775 in Person, North Carolina. He had one child with Unity Sarratt and two other children. He died in 1841 in Tennessee at the age of sixty-six.

1. William "Buck" Broadaway 1804-1877 (SM), White Store, Anson & Marshville, Union, NC (Creasie Broadaway, 1827)
2. King Broadaway 1844-1930 Lanesboro & Marshville, Anson, NC
3. John David King Broadaway 1883-1948, Lanesboro & Marshville, Anson, NC
4. Joe Broadaway 1917-1993, Union & Rockingham, NC
5. Joe Fred Broadaway, Lanesboro, Anson, NC

Parents
John (Jesse) Broadaway 1755–1841
Agnes Elizabeth Wilson 1758–1839

Siblings
James Broadaway Slave Master-18 1775–1862
Joseph Broadaway 1780–1842

Elizabeth Broadaway 1790–
John Broadaway Jr 1792–1841
Lemuel Broadaway Slave Master-13 1793–1873
Charlotte Broadaway 1794–1852
Lydia Broadaway 1796–1881
Sarah Sally Broadaway 1798–1857
Mary Broadaway 1800–1843

John Green Broadaway 1815–   Unity Serratt 1768–1858

Children
James Broadaway 1797–
Yancey Broadaway 1801–1884
Half siblings   William "Buck" Broadaway SM
James Johnathon Broadaway 1795–   1804–1877
Robin Thomas Broadaway 1797–   Frances Broadaway 1817–
1876   Sarah Broadaway 1820–
Annis Broadaway 1803–1881   Mary Broadaway
Rev. John Broadaway 1811–1870   John G Broadaway
Jeremiah B Broadaway 1817–1861   William "SM" Barrett 1800–1883
Spouse

**Global, Find A Grave Index for Non-Burials, Burials at Sea, and other Select
Burial Locations, 1300s-Current**

Name	Jesse Broadaway
Birth Date	1774
Birthplace	Person County, North Carolina, United States of America
Death Date	1840
Death Place	Lincoln County, Tennessee, United States of America
Has Bio?	N
Spouse	Unity Broadaway

Millennium File

Name	Jesse Broadway
Birth Date	1780
Birthplace	North Carolina, USA
Death Date	Dec 1841
Mother	Agnes

North Carolina Marriage Bonds, 1741-1868

Name	Jesse Broadaway
Gender	Male
Spouse	Unity Serratt
Spouse Gender	Female
Bond date	10 Dec 1799
Bond #	000106788
Marriage Date	19 Dec 1858

Level Info	NC Marriage Bonds, 1741-1868
Image Num	007117
County Person	
Record #	01 016
Bondsman	John Broadaway
Witness	William Hicks
Performed By	James King

U.S., Find A Grave Index, 1700s-Current

Name	Jesse Broadaway
Birth Date	1774
Birthplace	Person County, North Carolina
Death Date	1840
Death Place	Lincoln County, Tennessee
Has Bio?	N

War of 1812 Service Records

Name	Jesse Broadaway
Company	Davis's Battalion, West Tennessee, and North Carolina
Militia.	
Rank - Induction	Private
Rank - Discharge	Private
Roll Box	25
Microfilm Publication	M602

***

Slave Masters Introduced With One Branch of Slave Ancestors - Featured in Section III:

1. Jesse Broadaway 1775-1841, Slave Master, Person, NC & Lincoln, TN
2. William "Buck" Broadaway 1804-1877, Slave Master, White Store, Anson & Marshville, Union, NC
3. Creasie Broadaway 1827, Slave, White Store Township, Anson County, NC
4. King Broadaway 1844-1930, Slave, Lanesboro & Marshville, Anson, NC
5. John David King Broadaway 1883-1948, Lanesboro & Marshville, Anson, NC
6. Joe Broadaway 1917-1993, Union & Rockingham, NC
7. Joe Fred Broadaway, Lanesboro, Anson, NC & Clarksville, TN
8. Tammy J. Broadaway, Lanesboro, Anson, NC

William "Buck" Broadaway (SM) 1804-1877

BIRTH 06 SEP 1804 • White Store, Anson, NC
DEATH 15 JAN 1877 • Marshville Township (north part), Union, NC

When William "Buck" Broadaway was born on September 6, 1804, in White Store, North Carolina, his father, Jesse, was twenty-nine and his mother, Unity, was thirty-six. He married Sarah Marsh, and they had one daughter together. He also had one son with Harriett "Creasie" Broadaway. He then married Sarah Ann Gaddy and they had fourteen children together. He died on January 15, 1877, in Marshville, North Carolina, at the age of seventy-two.

Parents
Jesse Broadaway 1775–1841
Unity Serratt 1768–1858

Spouse
Sarah Marsh 1810–1847
Children
Martha Jane Broadaway 1826–1875

Spouse
Sarah Ann Gaddy 1824–1894
Children
John W Broadaway 1836–
William Marshal Broadaway 1839–1896
Joel F. Broadaway 1849–1850
J T Broadaway 1849–
Sarah Eugenia Broadaway 1852–1934
Walter L Broadaway 1853–1902
Christopher C Broadaway 1854–1887
Jeptha Gaddy Broadaway 1856–1892
Isham Broadaway 1857–
Helen Broadaway 1858–1934
Eliza "Ella" Broadaway 1860–1906
Mary Lilla Broadaway 1863–1915
Anna Broadaway 1864–1944

Francis C Broadaway 1864–1944

Spouse
Harriett "Creasie" Broadaway 1823–
Children
King Broadaway 1844–1930
Parents:
Jesse Broadaway SM 1775–1841
Unity Sarratt (Barrett) 1768–1858

Spouse:
Sarah Marsh 1810–1847

Children:
Martha Jane Broadaway 1826–1875

Spouse:
Sarah Ann Gaddy 1824–1894

Children:
James Marshall Broadaway 1824–1863
John W Broadaway 1836–1863
William Marshal Broadaway 1839–1896
Joel F. Broadaway 1849–1850

J T Broadaway 1849–
William L Broadaway 1851–1902
Sarah Eugenia Broadaway 1852–1934
Christopher C Broadaway 1854–1887
Jeptha Gaddy Broadaway 1856–1892
Isham Broadaway 1857–
Helen Broadaway 1858–1934
Eliza E "Ella" Broadaway 1860–1906
Mary Lilla Broadaway 1863–1915
Anna Broadaway 1864–1944
Francis Crander Broadaway 1866–1947

Spouse:
Creasie "Harriett" Broadway 1827–
(Slave)
Children:
King Broadway 1844–1930 (Slave)

Half Siblings:
James Broadaway
William "SM" Barrett

1850 United States Federal Census

Name   William Broadaway
Gender Male
Race   White
Age   45
Birth Year   abt 1805
Birthplace   North Carolina
Home in 1850   Diamond Hill, Anson, NC
Occupation   Farmer
IndustryAgriculture
Real Estate   3600
Line Number   36
Dwelling Number   852
Family Number 852
Inferred Spouse Sarah A Broadaway
Household members
Name   Age
William Broadaway   45
Sarah A Broadaway   25
James Broadaway   16

John Broadaway 14
William M Broadaway   11

Joel F Broadaway   1

1860 U.S. Federal Census - Slave Schedules

Name   Wm Broadaway
Residence Date 1860
Residence Place Meltonsville, Anson, NC
Number of Enslaved People   14
Role   Slave Owner
Household members
Gender Age
Female 38
Female 37
Male   21
Male   20
Male   16
Male   14
Male   12
Female 12
Male   9
Male   9
Male   8
Female 6
Female 4

1860 United States Federal Census

Name   William Broadaway
Age   55
Birth Year   abt 1805
Gender   Male
Race   White
Birthplace   North Carolina
Home in 1860   Meltonsville, Anson,
North Carolina
Post Office   White Store
Dwelling Number   518
Family Number   478
Occupation   Farmer
Real Estate Value   1500
Personal Estate Value   15000
Inferred Spouse S A Broadaway
Inferred Child   J T Broadaway
Household members
Name   Age
William Broadaway 55
S A Broadaway   35
J T Broadaway   1
W L Broadaway 9
C C Broadaway   6
S E Broadaway   8
J Broadaway   4
H Broadaway   2
E E Broadaway 3/12

1870 United States Federal Census

Name   William Broadaway
Age in 1870   65
Birth Date   abt 1805
Birthplace   North Carolina
Dwelling Number 103
Home in 1870   White Store, Anson,
North Carolina
Race   White
Gender   Male
Post Office   Wadesboro
Occupation   Farmer
Male Citizen Over 21   Yes
Personal Estate Value   600
Real Estate Value   1900
Inferred Spouse Sarah Broadaway
Inferred Children   Walter L
Broadaway
Household members
Name   Age
William Broadaway   65
Sarah Broadaway   46
Walter L Broadaway   17
Eugenia Broadaway   17
Christopher Broadaway 16
Isham Broadaway   13
Hellen Broadaway   11
Ella Broadaway 9
Mary Broadaway7
Anah Broadaway   5
Francis Broadaway   2

American Civil War Soldiers
Name   **William Broadaway**
Residence   Anson County, North Carolina
Occupation   Artist

Enlistment Date 22 May 1861
Enlistment Place Anson County, North Carolina
Side Served   Confederacy
State Served   North Carolina
Sources 16

American Civil War Soldiers

Name	**William Broadaway**
Residence	Anson County, North Carolina
Enlistment Date	1 Jul 1861
Enlistment Place	Anson County, North Carolina
Side Served	Confederacy
State Served	North Carolina
Sources 16	

***

Slave Masters Introduced and One Branch of Slave Ancestors

1. Jesse Broadaway 1775-1841, Slave Master, Person, NC & Lincoln, TN
2. William "Buck" Broadaway 1804-1877, Slave Master, White Store, Anson & Marshville, Union, NC
3. Creasie Broadaway 1827, Slave, White Store Township, Anson County, NC
4. King Broadaway 1844-1930, Slave, Lanesboro & Marshville, Anson, NC
5. John David King Broadaway 1883-1948, Lanesboro & Marshville, Anson, NC
6. Joe Broadaway 1917-1993, Union & Rockingham, NC
7. Joe Fred Broadaway, Lanesboro, Anson, NC & Clarksville, TN
8. Tammy J. Broadaway, Lanesboro, Anson, NC

Section III Jesse Broadaway 1775-1841, Person Co., NC (Slave Master)

1. William "Buck" Broadaway 1804-1877 (Slave Master) & Creasie Broadaway 1827
2. Creasie Broadaway 1827 Meltonsville & White Store Township, Anson, NC (John Barrett)
3. Marshall C. Broadaway 1847 (Elizabeth-Bettie) Lilesville & Lanesboro, Anson, NC
4. Orlander L. Broadaway 1884-1949 (Broadway), North Carolina, Hampton & Moro, AR
5. Elbert Buster Broadway 1911-2000, Hampton & Moro, AR

6. Lenora Broadway Wilder, Moro, AR, Chicago, IL

***

Creasie "Harriett" Broadway (Slave) 1827–

Birth: 1827•White Store Township, Anson County, North Carolina
Death: Unknown

Creasie Broadway was born in 1827 in White Store, North Carolina. She had one child with William "Buck" Broadaway and four other children. She moved five times during her lifetime. She lived in Anson, North Carolina, in 1860 and moved to Sandy Ridge, North Carolina, by 1900. In 1870 Creasie lived in White Store, Anson, North Carolina. Additionally, Creasie worked as a housekeeper and in 1880, she lived in the same area as a widower.

Spouse/Partner: William "Buck" Broadaway SM 1804–1877
Children:
1. King Broadaway 1844–1930
2. Marshall C Broadaway 1847–, Lilesville, Anson, NC
3. Jacob "Dock" Brilliant Broadaway 1848–
4. Alexander Broadaway 1851–1924, Lanesboro & Peachland, Anson, NC
5. Alphonzo Broadaway 1853– Anson & Lanesboro; Near Peachland, Anson, NC

Spouse: John Barrett 1823– John Barrett married Creasie in 1848
Children:
1. *Marshall C Broadway 1847–1890*
2. *Jacob "Dock" Brilliant Broadway 1848–*
3. *Alexander Broadway 1851–1924*
4. Andrew Barrett 1852–
5. *Alphonzo Broadway 1853–*
6. Caroline Barrett 1860–
7. Ben F Barrett 1860–
8. Ellis Barrett 1861–1925
9. John Barrett Jr 1864–1888
10. Evalina Barrett 1869–1931

King Broadaway's 1844-1930 Ancestors and Descendants

When King Broadway was born in May 1844 in Lanesboro, North Carolina, his father, William, was thirty-nine and his mother, Creasie, was seventeen. He married Ellen

14

Shavers, and they had five children together. He then married Hattie Lockhart and they had one daughter together. He died in 1930 in his hometown at the age of eighty-six, and was buried in Brooklyn, New York.

Grandparents:
Jesse Broadaway 1775-1841
Unity Sarrett 1788-1858

Parents:
William "Buck" Broadaway SM 1804–1877
Creasie "Harriett" Broadway (Slave) 1827–

Spouse:
Ellen Shavers 1852–1882

Children:
Sarah Elizabeth "Bettie" Broadway 1876–1958
Ann Eliza Broadway 1878–1952
Mary Florence Broadway 1881–1965
John David "King" Broadway 1883–1948
Julius Broadway 1887–1963

Spouse:
Hattie Lockhart 1864–1943

Children:
Wincy Broadway 1881–1917

Timeline of King Broadaway
- 1860, King, Black, 16 slaves owned by William Broadway
- 1870, King, White, 48 & Catherine Newberry 48, Lanesboro, NC
- 1880, King, Mulatto, 33, Farmer, Married, but wife not living at residence
- 1900, King, Black, 56, Marshville, Union, Own home-free of mortgage, Married-Hattie
- 1910, King, Mulatto, 66, Marshville, Married-Hattie 54
- 1920, King, Black, 75, Lanesboro, Anson, Widowed, living with John & Ada Broadaway family & kids

The State of North Carolina,   No.

_____ COUNTY.

To any ordained Minister of any Religious Denomination, or to any Justice of the Peace, for said county. _____ having applied to me for a license for the marriage of *King Broadaway*, of *Lanesboro Township*, aged *28* years, color *colored*, son of *William Broadaway*, and *Harriet Broadaway*, and *of whom both are living*, and reside at *Lanesboro*, in the State of *North Carolina*, and *Ellen Showers*, aged *22* years, color *colored*, daughter of *George Showers*, and *Mary Showers*, and *of whom both are living*, and reside at *Lanesboro Township*, in the State of *North Carolina*.

And the written consent of _____ having been filed with me, and there being no legal impediment to such Marriage known to me, you are hereby authorized and licensed within one year from the date hereof, to celebrate and solemnize the proposed Marriage at any place within the said County. You are required within two months after you have celebrated such Marriage, to return this license to me, at my office with your signature subscribed to the certificate under this license, the blanks therein filled according to the facts, under the penalty of forfeiting two hundred dollars to the use of any person who shall sue for the same.

Issued this *1st* day of *Sept* A. D. 187 *6*.

John David "King" Broadaway 1873-1948 Ancestors
BIRTH 6 JAN 1873 • Lanesboro, Anson, North Carolina, USA
DEATH 29 SEP 1948 • Marshville, Union, North Carolina, USA

When John David "King" Broadway was born on January 6, 1883, in Lanesboro, North Carolina, his father, King, was thirty-eight and his mother, Ellen, was thirty-one. He married Tabitha Lotharp, and they had four children together. He then married Ada Staton and they had twelve children together. He died on September 29, 1948, in Marshville, North Carolina, at the age of sixty-five, and was buried in White Store, North Carolina.

John David King Ancestors

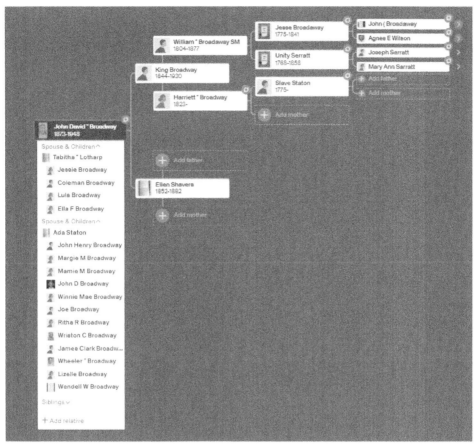

John David "King" Broadaway Ancestors and Descendants

Great-Grandparents of John David "King" Broadway
Jesse Broadaway 1775–1841
Unity Sarratt 1768–1858

Grandparents of John David "King" Broadway
William "Buck" Broadaway, Slave Master, 1804–1877 (Possible)
Creasie "Harriett" Broadway 1827–
Parents of John David "King" Broadway
King Broadway 1844–1930, Mulatto, 33, Farmer
Ellen Shavers 1852–1882, Mulatto, 28

Siblings

Sarah Elizabeth "Bettie" Broadway 1876–1958
Ann Eliza Broadway 1878–1952
Mary Florence Broadway 1881–1965
Julius Broadway 1887–1963

Half siblings
Wincy Broadway 1881–1917Spouse

Spouse
Tabitha Lotharp 1876–1907
Children
Jessie Broadway 1897–
Coleman Broadway 1899–1973
Lula Broadway 1900–1976
Ella Frances Broadway 1901–1973

Spouse
Ada Staton 1886–1931

Children
John Henry Broadway Jr 1902–1986
Margie Melissa Broadway 1909–1998
Mamie M Broadway 1912–2006
John D Broadway 1914–1996
Winnie Mae Broadway 1916–
Joe Broadway 1917–1993
Retha Rosetta Broadway 1919–1993
Wriston Cane Broadway 1919–2009
James Clark Broadway 1924–1999
Wheeler "Charles" Broadway 1925–1973
Lizelle Broadway 1926–
Wendell Wikie Broadway 1928–1991

Joe Broadaway 1917-1993 Ancestors and Descendants

When Joe Broadway was born on June 22, 1917, his father, John of Lanesboro, was thirty-four and his mother, Ada, was thirty. He married Mable Lindsey in Chesterfield, South Carolina. They had four children in seventeen years. Joe worked at a Sawmill. He died on October 3, 1993, in Rockingham, North Carolina, at the age of seventy-six, and was buried in Polkton, North Carolina.

Great-Grandparents of Joe Broadway (SM)
Jesse Broadaway 1775–1841
Unity Sarratt 1768–1858

Grandparents of Joe Broadway (SM)
William "Buck" Broadaway, Slave Master, 1804–1877 (Calculated Partner)
Creasie "Harriett" Broadway 1827–

Parents of Joe Broadway
King Broadway 1844–1930
Ellen Shavers 1852–1882

Spouse of Joe Broadaway
Joe Broadway 1873–1948
Ada Staton 1886–1931

Siblings
John Henry Broadway Jr 1902–1986
Margie Melissa Broadway 1909–1998
Mamie M Broadway 1912–2006
John D Broadway 1914–1996
Winnie Mae Broadway 1916–
Retha Rosetta Broadway 1919–1993
Wriston Cane Broadway 1919–2009
James Clark Broadway 1924–1999
Wheeler "Charles" Broadway 1925–1973
Lizelle Broadway 1926–
Wendell Wikie Broadway 1928–1991

Half siblings
Jessie Broadway 1897–
Coleman Broadway 1899–1973
Lula Broadway 1900–1976
Ella Frances Broadway 1901–1973

Spouse of Joe Broadaway
Mable Lindsey 1922–1997

Children

Joe Fred Broadaway 1950–
Gwendolyn Marie Broadway 1953–1978
Deborah Ann Broadway 1957
Sharon Joyce Broadway 1967–

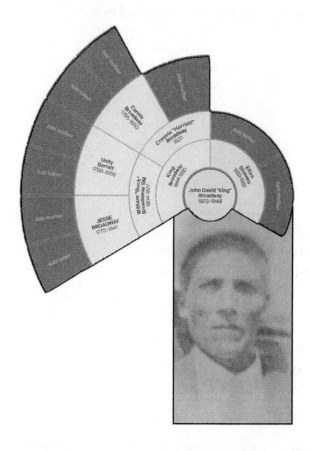

Joe Fred Broadaway Ancestors and Descendants

When Joe Fred Broadaway was born in Anson, North Carolina, his father, Joe, was thirty-two and his mother, Mable, was twenty-seven. He had two sons and one daughter with Ruby J Tillman between 1969 and 1972. He had three sisters.

Tree Overview

'Broadway' Family Tree The "Broadway Tree" is a work in progress. It is composed largely of direct descendants of former slave, James Broadway. All the black Broadway descendants have been changed to spell "Broadway" not Broadaway.

Great²-Grandparents of Joe Fred Broadaway

Jesse Broadaway 1775–1841
Unity Sarratt 1768–1858

Great Grandparents of Joe Fred Broadaway

William "Buck" Broadaway, Slave Master, 1804–1877 (Possible)
Creasie "Harriett" Broadway 1827–

Grandparents of Joe Fred Broadaway

King Broadway 1844–1930
Ellen Shavers 1852–1882

Parents of Joe Fred Broadaway

Joe Broadaway
Mable Lindsey 1922–1997

Siblings of Joe Fred Broadaway

Gwendolyn Marie Broadway 1953–1978
Deborah Ann Broadway 1957–
Sharon Joyce Broadway 1967–

Spouse of Joe Fred Broadaway

Ruby J Tillman 1950–

Children of Joe Fred Broadaway

Derek Chauncey Tillman 1969–
Tammy Juanete Broadaway 1970–
Antwan Deontony Broadaway 1972–2021

SECTION IV CREASIE BROADWAY

Broadaway Family History Trivia: During 1800s there was a high infant and childhood death rate, the average life expectancy of a slave at birth was just 21 or 22 years, compared to 40 to 43 years for antebellum whites. Compared to whites, relatively few slaves lived into old age

Creasie Broadway was born in 1827 in White Store, North Carolina. She had one child with William "Buck" Broadaway and four other children. She moved five times during her lifetime. She lived in Anson, North Carolina in 1860. In 1870 and 1880, Creasie lived in White Store, Anson, North Carolina. Additionally, Creasie worked as a housekeeper. In 1880, she was listed as a widower. By 1900, she moved to Sandy Ridge, North Carolina.

Probable Partner: William "Buck" Broadaway SM 1804–1877
Children:
1. King Broadaway 1844–1930

Spouse: John Barrett 1823- (John Barrett married Creasie in 1848)
Children:
1. *Marshall C Broadway 1847–1890,* Lilesville, Anson, NC
2. *Jacob "Dock" Brilliant Broadway 1848–*
3. *Alexander Broadway 1851–1924,* Lanesboro & Peachland, Anson, NC
4. Andrew Barrett 1852–
5. *Alphonzo Broadway 1853–,* Anson & Lanesboro; Near Peachland, Anson, NC
6. Caroline Barrett 1860–
7. Ben F Barrett 1860–

8. Ellis Barrett 1861–1925
9. John Barrett Jr 1864–1888
10. Evalina Barrett 1869–1931

North Carolina Marriage

Name	Harrett Barrett
Gender	Female
Race	Black
Spouse	John Barrett
Spouse Gender	Male
Spouse Race	Black
Marriage Date	1848
Marriage County	Union
Marriage State	North Carolina

1860 U.S. Federal Census - Slave Schedules

Gender	Female
Race	Black
Age	37
Birth Date	abt 1823
Residence Date	1860
Residence Place	Meltonsville, Anson, NC
Role	Slave
Slave Owner	Wm Broadaway

Household members

Gender	Age
Female	38
Female	37
Male	21
Male	20
Male	16
Male	14
Male	12
Female	12

Male	9
Male	9
Male	8
Female	6
Female	4
Male	2
Close	

1870 United States Federal Census

Name	Creacy Braudaway
Age in 1870	43
Birth Date	abt 1827
Birthplace	North Carolina
Dwelling #	242
Home in 1870	White Store, Anson, NC
Race	Black
Gender	Female
Post Office	Wadesboro
Occupation	Keeping House
Cannot Read	Yes
Cannot Write	Yes

Household members

Name	Age
Aly Braudaway	
Creacy Braudaway	43

1880 United States Federal Census

Name	Creacy Broadaway
Age	54
Birth Date	Abt 1826
Birthplace	North Carolina
Home in 1880	Whites Store,

Anson, NC

Dwelling #	91
Race	Black
Gender	Female
Marital Status	Widowed
Father's Birthplace	NC
Mother's Birthplace	NC
Occupation	House ...
Cannot Read	Y
Cannot Write	Y
Neighbors	View others on page.

Household members

Name	Age
Creacy Broadaway	54

1900 United States Federal Census

Name	Harriet Barrett
Age	80
Birth Date	
Birthplace	North Carolina, USA
Home in 1900	Sandy Ridge, Union, NC
Ward of City	4904
Sheet Number	5
Number of Dwelling in Order of Visitation	80

Family Number 81

Race	Black
Gender	Female
Relation to Head of House	Mother
Marital Status	Widowed
Father's Birthplace	NC
Mother's Birthplace	NC
Can Read	N
Can Write	N
Can Speak English	Y
Neighbors	View others on page

Household members

Name	Age
Harriet Barrett	80
Caroline Barrett	40
John C Barrett	14
Sis Barrett	5
Mamie Barrett	4
Close	

North Carolina Death Certificates, 1909-1975

Name	Creasie Broadaway
Gender	Female
Birthplace	Anson County
Spouse	John Barrett
Child	Alexander Broadaway, died 1925

Alexander Broadaway 1851-1924

Birth: 03 Feb 1851•Anson, White Store, Anson, NC
Death: 09 May 1924•Lanesboro; Near Peachland, Anson, NC

When Alexander Broadway was born on February 3, 1851, in White Store, North Carolina, his father, John, was twenty-six and his mother, Creasie, was twenty-four. He married Isabella Huntly on August 22, 1871, in Anson, North Carolina. He then married Mary L Covington and they had ten children together. He died on May 9, 1924, at the age of seventy-three.

Parents:
William Buck Broadaway/John Barrett 1825–
Creasie Broadway 1827–

Spouses/Partners:
Isabella Huntly 1852–1901
Mary L Covington 1876–1963

Children:
Mary Roanna Broadway 1898–1963
William Elijha Broadway 1900–1971
Andrew B Broadway 1901–1975
Alexander A Broadway 1904–1969
Walter L Broadway 1906–1932
Mittie Broadway 1908–1979
Francis A Broadway 1911–
Booker W Broadway 1914–1971
Fletcher Haywood Broadway 1917–1971
Woodrow Willison Broadway 1920–

William Elijha Broadway 1900-1971
Birth: 23 Dec 1900 • North Carolina, USA
Death: Nov 1971 • District of Columbia, DC

Marshall C. Broadaway 1847-1890

When Marshall C Broadway was born in 1847 in Lilesville, North Carolina, his father, John, was twenty-two and his mother, Creasie, was twenty. He had four sons and three daughters with Elizabeth Shavers between 1874 and 1889. He died in 1890 in Hampton, Arkansas, at the age of forty-three.

Timeline of Marshall Broadaway:
- 1870 Worked on Railroad at same time as Sandy Clark; Lived in a boarding house with ten young men.

- 1880 Married 1875. Lived in Lanesboro, Anson, NC with wife, Elizabeth (Bettie) twenty-six and two children: Robert five and Charlotte three.
- 1890 No records in Lee County, AR because of a fire. Also, Ellace 1886 and Susie 1889 Broadway were born. It is assumed that Marshall C. Broadway died between 1889-1900.
- 1900 Bettie Broadway was widowed and had a mortgage on a farm in Hampton, Lee, AR.
- 1910 & 1910 Bettie Broadway no longer had a farm. She worked as a cook for private families.
- 1920 Bettie Joiner James lived with son, James (Jim) Broadway and family.

Parents:
William Buck Broadaway/John Barrett 1825–
Creasie "Harriett" Broadway 1827–

Spouse:
Unknown
Elizabeth Shavers 1847–1929

Children:
Bob "Robert" Broadway 1874–1920
Charlott Broadway 1875–1938
James Broadway 1878–
Ellis Broadway 1881–1949
Orlander Lane Broadway 1884–1949
Ellace Broadway 1886–
Susie Broadway 1889–1926

Orlander Lane Broadway 1884-1949

When Orlander Lane Broadway was born on October 10, 1884, in North Carolina, his father, Marshall, was thirty-seven and his mother, Elizabeth, was thirty-seven. He married Sarah Augusta Clark, and they had eleven children together. He also had one daughter with Carrie Mables. He died on April 11, 1949, in Moro, Arkansas, at the age of sixty-three, and was buried there.

Parents:
Marshall C Broadway 1847–1890
Elizabeth Shavers 1847–1929

Spouse:
Sarah Augusta Clark 1888–1933
Children:
Eula Broadway 1907–1990
Darthula (Dorothy) Broadway 1910–
Elbert Buster Broadway 1911–2000
Thomas R. Broadway 1913–1984
Eddie Broadway 1916–1916
Cuba Broadway 1917–1987
Herbert Broadway 1920–1920
Joe Nathan Broadway 1921–1962
Quincy Thomas "QT" (Bull)
Broadway 1923–1994
J T Broadway 1929–1931
L D Broadway 1931–1932

Partner:
Carrie Mables 1904–
Children:
Elizabeth Broadway 1927–2020

Spouse:
Pearl Mary Hall 1891–1959

family
is a gift that lasts
forever

Elbert Buster Broadway 1911–2000

When Elbert Buster Broadway was born on October 5, 1911, in Moro, Arkansas, his father, Orlander, was twenty-six and his mother, Sarah, was twenty-two. He married Maria Louise "Red" Smith on December 25, 1935, in his hometown. They had two children during their marriage. He died on February 12, 2000, in his hometown at the age of eighty-eight, and was buried there.

Parents
Orlander Lane Broadway 1884–1949
Sarah Augusta Clark 1888–1933

Spouse
Maria Louise "Red" Smith 1910–1998
Children
Linnie Broadway 1936–1936
Lenora "Peter" Broadway 1937–

Lenora Broadway Wilder

When Lenora "Peter" Broadway was born on November 15, 1937, in Lee, Arkansas, her father, Elbert, was twenty-six, and her mother, Maria, was twenty-seven. She had three sons and one daughter with Troy K. Wilder between 1958 and 1964. She had one sister. Resident of Lee County, Arkansas and then, Cook, Chicago, Illinois

Parents
Elbert Buster Broadway 1911–2000
Maria Louise "Red" Smith 1910–1998

Spouse
Troy K. Wilder 1939–2019
Children
Larry Wilder 1958–
Sharon Wilder 1960–
Derek E Wilder 1962–
Brian Wilder 1964–

family is a gift that lasts forever

SECTION V: FIVE BROADAWAY SIBLINGS MYSTERY SOLVED

Broadaway Family History Trivia: *Ancestor Marshall Broadway worked on North Carolina Railroad in Anson County along with Sandy Clark, who later became brother-in-law. At one point, post Emancipation according to a US Census, the five siblings lived near each other in the same neighborhood.*

The Broadway slave siblings connected in the Broadaway Mystery are James, Robert "Bob", Harry, Harriet "Creasie", and George Broadway. (See below) They belonged to the same *slave owner* at one time or the other. The Broadway slaves were from Anson County. For each of the Broadway slaves, no parents are directly documented. Additionally, all slave siblings are found in the 1870 and 1880 United States Federal Census in Anson County, North Carolina. Additionally on the Census, they are listed as Black, Mulatto, White, but mostly as Black.

1.   James A Baucom-Broadway 1815–1881
2.   Harry Broadway 1815–1887
3.   Robert "Bob" Broadway 1817–1881
4.   Creasie "Harriett" Broadway 1827–
5.   George Broadway 1835–

James home, according to the 1870 and 1880 Census, was Burnsville to Lanesboro; Robert "Bob" and Harry lived in Ansonville during 1870 and 1880. George home during 1870 and 1880 was Lanesboro to Ansonville. Harriet "Creasie" live in White Store Township in 1870 and 1880, then moved to Sandy Ridge, Union, North Carolina as seen in the 1900 Census.

James and Harry had "inferred children" listed on the 1870 Census. James had one inferred child named Marshall B. Broadway. Harry had an inferred spouse: Eliza Broadway and several inferred children: Adline, Sam, Marshall, Julie, Julie, and Eliza Broadway.

Occupation for James was farm laborer during 1870 and 1880. Robert worked on the railroad according to the 1870 Census and 1880 as a laborer. Harry and George were farm laborers in 1870 and farmers in 1880. Harriet's occupation in 1870 and 1880 was housekeeper.

James had his second inferred wife, Margaret, living with him in 1870 and was a widower in 1880. Robert married an older woman, Harriet "Miney". He was with her during the 1870 and 1880 Census. Harry had been with his inferred wife, Eliza, since 1840 and legally married Eliza in 1865. On the 1870 and 1880 Census, Eliza was still his wife.

However, according to a marriage certificate, Harry married Milly Forest in 1867. According to North Carolina Marriage Collection 1741-2004, Harriett Barrett married John Barrett in 1848 in Union County. However, Harriett had children with the name Broadway and Barrett. On the 1880 and 1900 Census, Harriett is listed as widowed. Additionally, in 1870 George had an inferred spouse, Harriet, and on the 1880 Census, George was still married to Harriett.

Based on the Ancestry.com findings, James, Robert "Bob", Harry, Harriet "Creasie", and George Broadway are Broadway Slave Siblings.

Father: Cannis Broadaway 1795-1850

A family of five siblings, currently, researching Cannis Broadway as being the father of the five Broadway slave siblings below. Cannis Broadway was born in 1795 in Polkton, North Carolina. He may have had four sons and one daughter between 1815 and 1835. He died in 1850 in his hometown at the age of fifty-five.

Spouse: Unknown

Children:
1.   James A Baucom-Broadway 1815–1881
2.   Harry Broadway 1815–1887
3.   Robert "Bob" Broadway 1817–1881
4.   Creasie "Harriett" Broadway 1827–
5.   George Broadway 1835–

Section IV Creasie Broadaway 1827 – (Wm Broadaway & John Barrett)

Birth: 1827•White Store Township, Anson County, North Carolina
Death: Unknown

Creasie Broadway was born in 1827 in White Store, North Carolina. She had one child with William "Buck" Broadaway and four other children. She moved five times during her lifetime. She lived in Anson, North Carolina in 1860. In 1870 and 1880, Creasie lived in White Store,

Anson, North Carolina. Additionally, Creasie worked as a housekeeper. In 1880, she was listed as a widower. By 1900, she moved to Sandy Ridge, North Carolina.

Probable Partner: William "Buck" Broadaway SM 1804–1877
Children:
1.   King Broadaway 1844–1930

Spouse: John Barrett 1823- (John Barrett married Creasie in 1848)

Children:
1.   Marshall C Broadway 1847–1890, Lilesville, Anson, NC
2.   Jacob "Dock" Brilliant Broadway 1848–
3.   Alexander Broadway 1851–1924, Lanesboro & Peachland, Anson, NC
4.   Andrew Barrett 1852–
5.   Alphonzo Broadway 1853–, Anson & Lanesboro; Near Peachland, Anson, NC
6.   Caroline Barrett 1860–
7.   Ben F Barrett 1860–
8.   Ellis Barrett 1861–1925
9.   John Barrett Jr 1864–1888
10.   Evalina Barrett 1869–1931

North Carolina Marriage
Name	Harrett Barrett
Gender	Female
Race	Black
Spouse	John Barrett
Spouse Gender	Male
Spouse Race	Black
Marriage Date	1848
Marriage County	Union
Marriage State	North Carolina

1860 U.S. Federal Census - Slave Schedules
Gender	Female
Race	Black
Age	37
Birth Date	abt 1823
Residence Date	1860
Residence Place	Meltonsville, Anson, NC
Role	Slave
Slave Owner	Wm Broadaway
Household members	

Gender Age

Female 38

Female 37

Male   21

Male   20

Male   16

Male   14

Male   12

Female 12

Male   9

Male   9

Male   8

Female 6

Female 4

Male   2

Close

1870 United States Federal Census

Name	Creacy Braudaway
Age in 1870	43
Birth Date	abt 1827
Birthplace	North Carolina
Dwelling #	242
Home in 1870	White Store, Anson, NC
Race	Black
Gender	Female
Post Office	Wadesboro
Occupation	Keeping House
Cannot Read	Yes
Cannot Write	Yes

Household members

Name	Age
Aly Braudaway	
Creacy Braudaway	43

1880 United States Federal Census

Name	Creacy Broadaway
Age	54
Birth Date	Abt 1826
Birthplace	North Carolina
Home in 1880	Whites Store, Anson, NC
Dwelling #	91

Race   Black
Gender   Female
Marital Status Widowed
Father's Birthplace   NC
Mother's Birthplace   NC
Occupation   House ...
Cannot Read   Y
Cannot Write   Y
Neighbors   View others on page.
Household members
Name   Age
Creacy Broadaway   54

1900 United States Federal Census
Name   Harriet Barrett
Age   80
Birth Date
Birthplace   North Carolina, USA
Home in 1900   Sandy Ridge, Union, NC
Ward of City   4904
Sheet Number   5
Number of Dwelling in Order of Visitation 80
Family Number 81
Race   Black
Gender Female
Relation to Head of House Mother
Marital Status   Widowed
Father's Birthplace   NC
Mother's Birthplace   NC
Can Read   N
Can Write   N
Can Speak English   Y
Neighbors   View others on page
Household members
Name   Age
Harriet Barrett 80
Caroline Barrett 40
John C Barrett 14
Sis Barrett   5
Mamie Barrett   4
Close

North Carolina Death Certificates, 1909-1975

Name	Creasie Broadaway
Gender	Female
Birthplace	Anson County
Spouse	John Barrett
Child	Alexander Broadaway, died 1925

Alexander Broadaway 1851-1924

Birth:03 Feb 1851•Anson, White Store, Anson, NC
Death:09 May 1924•Lanesboro; Near Peachland, Anson, NC

When Alexander Broadway was born on February 3, 1851, in White Store, North Carolina, his father, John, was twenty-six and his mother, Creasie, was twenty-four. He married Isabella Huntly on August 22, 1871, in Anson, North Carolina. He then married Mary L Covington and they had ten children together. He died on May 9, 1924, at the age of seventy-three.

Parents:
William Buck Broadaway/John Barrett 1825–
Creasie Broadaway 1827–

Spouses/Partners:
Isabella Huntly 1852–1901
Mary L Covington 1876–1963

Children:
Mary Roanna Broadway 1898–1963
William Elijha Broadway 1900–1971
Andrew B Broadway 1901–1975
Alexander A Broadway 1904–1969
Walter L Broadway 1906–1932
Mittie Broadway 1908–1979
Francis A Broadway 1911–
Booker W Broadway 1914–1971
Fletcher Haywood Broadway 1917–1971
Woodrow Willison Broadway 1920–

William Elijha Broadway 1900-1971
Birth: 23 Dec 1900 • North Carolina, USA
Death: Nov 1971 • District of Columbia, DC

Marshall C. Broadaway 1847-1890

When Marshall C Broadway was born in 1847 in Lilesville, North Carolina, his father, John, was twenty-two and his mother, Creasie, was twenty. He had four sons and three daughters with Elizabeth Shavers between 1874 and 1889. He died in 1890 in Hampton, Arkansas, at the age of forty-three.

Marshall C. Broadaway Timeline:
- 1870 Worked on Railroad at same time as Sandy Clark; Lived in a boarding house with ten young men.
- 1880 Married 1875. Lived in Lanesboro, Anson, NC with wife, Elizabeth (Bettie) twenty-six and two children: Robert five and Charlotte three.
- 1890 No records in Lee County, AR because of a fire. Also, Ellace 1886 and Susie 1889 Broadway were born. It is assumed that Marshall C. Broadway died between 1889-1900.
- 1900 Bettie Broadway was widowed and had a mortgage on a farm in Hampton, Lee, AR.
- 1910 & 1910 Bettie Broadway no longer had a farm. She worked as a cook for private families.
- 1920 Bettie Joiner James lived with son, James (Jim) Broadway and family.

Parents:
William Buck Broadaway/John Barrett 1825–
Creasie "Harriett" Broadway 1827–

Spouse:
Unknown
Elizabeth Shavers 1847–1929

Children:
Bob "Robert" Broadway 1874–1920
Charlott Broadway 1875–1938
James Broadway 1878–
Ellis Broadway 1881–1949
Orlander Lane Broadway 1884–1949
Ellace Broadway 1886–
Susie Broadway 1889–1926

Orlander Lane Broadway 1884-1949

When Orlander Lane Broadway was born on October 10, 1884, in North Carolina, his father, Marshall, was thirty-seven and his mother, Elizabeth, was thirty-seven. He married Sarah

Augusta Clark, and they had eleven children together. He also had one daughter with Carrie Mables. He died on April 11, 1949, in Moro, Arkansas, at the age of sixty-three, and was buried.

Parents:
Marshall C Broadway 1847–1890
Elizabeth Shavers 1847–1929

Spouse:
Sarah Augusta Clark 1888–1933
Children:
Eula Broadway 1907–1990
Darthula (Dorothy) Broadway 1910–
Elbert Buster Broadway 1911–2000
Thomas R. Broadway 1913–1984
Eddie Broadway 1916–1916
Cuba Broadway 1917–1987
Herbert Broadway 1920–1920
Joe Nathan Broadway 1921–1962
Quincy Thomas "QT" (Bull) Broadway 1923–1994
J T Broadway 1929–1931
L D Broadway 1931–1932

Partner:
Carrie Mables 1904–

Children:
Elizabeth Broadway 1927–2020

Spouse:
Pearl Mary Hall 1891–1959

Elbert Buster Broadway 1911–2000
When Elbert Buster Broadway was born on October 5, 1911, in Moro, Arkansas, his father, Orlander, was twenty-six and his mother, Sarah, was twenty-two. He married Maria Louise "Red" Smith on December 25, 1935, in his hometown. They had two children during their marriage. He died on February 12, 2000, in his hometown at the age of eighty-eight, and was buried there.

Parents
Orlander Lane Broadway 1884–1949
Sarah Augusta Clark 1888–1933

Spouse
Maria Louise "Red" Smith 1910–1998
Children
Linnie Broadway 1936–1936
Lenora "Peter" Broadway 1937–

Lenora Broadway Wilder
When Lenora "Peter" Broadway was born on November 15, 1937, in Lee, Arkansas, her father, Elbert, was twenty-six, and her mother, Maria, was twenty-seven. She had three sons and one daughter with Troy K. Wilder between 1958 and 1964. She had one sister.
Resident of Lee County, Arkansas and then, Cook, Chicago, Illinois

Parents
Elbert Buster Broadway 1911–2000
Maria Louise "Red" Smith 1910–1998

Spouse
Troy K. Wilder 1939–2019
Children
Larry Wilder 1958–
Sharon Wilder 1960–
Derek E Wilder 1962–
Brian Wilder 1964–

family
is a gift that lasts
—forever—

40

SECTION VI HARRY BROADAWAY

In 1850, due to the railroad's construction, there was a very high demand for enslaved laborers during the mid-19th century in Western North Carolina. Enslaved people and later former slaves were assigned many tasks such as digging track beds, laying tracks, working as cleaners, brakemen, maintenance workers, and cooks. Family historians discovered Marshall B. Broadaway and Sandy Clark living in a boarding house for railroad employees.

When Harry Broadaway and his twin brother James A were born in 1815 in Ansonville, North Carolina, their father, Slave, was twenty. He married Eliza Broadaway, and they had seven children together. He then married Milly Forest and they had one daughter together. He died in 1887 in his hometown at age seventy-two.

Harry Broadaway 1815-1887 Ansonville, Anson, NC, 1870 Hanny Broadway, 1880 H. Broadaway, 1928 Broadaway
1. Hamilton Broadaway 1841-1880, Anson, NC; North, Orangeburg, South Carolina
2. Lewis Walter Broadaway 1863-1950, Burnsville, Anson, NC 1870-1950
3. Gaston Broadaway 1887-1924, Burnsville, Anson, NC 1900-1920/Clayton Broadaway Sr. 1904-1986, Burnsville, Anson, NC 1910-1950, Polkton, Anson, NC, Albemarle, Stanly, North Carolina 1986
4. Kenneth C. Broadaway 1919-1985, Oakboro, Stanley, NC, Salisbury, Rowan, NC
5. Roderick Craig Broadaway

Hamilton "Harry" Broadway 1841–1880

When Hamilton "Harry" Broadway was born in 1841 in North, Orangeburg, South Carolina, his father, Harry, was twenty-six and his mother, Eliza, was sixteen. He married Celia " Lelia" Ann George on June 11, 1871, in Anson, North Carolina. They had four children during their marriage. He died in 1880 in North Carolina at the age of thirty-nine.

Parents:
Harry Broadway 1815–1887
Eliza Broadway 1825–1887

Spouse:
Celia " Lelia" Ann George 1843–
Children:
Lewis Walter Broadway 1863–1950
John Hampton Broadway 1866–1963
Henry Clifer Broadway 1867–1953
Harriet Luvinia Broadway 1868–1973

Lewis Walter Broadaway 1863–1950

When Lewis Walter Broadaway was born on May 15, 1863, in Burnsville, North Carolina, his father, Hamilton, was twenty-two and his mother, Celia, was twenty. He married Edith Davis, and they had thirteen children together. He then married Laura Hasty, and they had three children together. He died on April 3, 1950, in his hometown at the age of eighty-six, and was buried in Polkton, North Carolina.

Parents:
Hamilton "Harry" Broadway 1841–1880
Celia " Lelia" Ann George 1843–

Spouse:
Edith Davis 1865–1928
Married: Mar 2, 1884, Stanly, NC
Children:
Gaston Broadaway 1887–1924
Martha Broadaway 1889–
Lola Broadaway 1890–1973
John Adam Broadaway 1893–1970
Minnie Broadaway 1895–1989
Mary E Broadaway 1896–1963
Bertha Broadaway 1896–1962

Charles R Broadaway 1899–1978

Ella Jane Broadaway 1902–2001

Sun B Broadaway 1903–1979

Henry J Broadaway 1903–1974

Clayton Broadaway Sr 1904–1986

Ida Flay Broadaway 1907–1990

Spouse:

Laura Hasty 1881–1961

Children:

Aman Broadaway 1915–

Geneva Broadaway 1920–

Arena Broadaway 1922–

Laura Hasty 1881–1961

BIRTH 10 JUN 1881 • Union County, North Carolina, USA

DEATH 01 SEPT 1961 • Monroe, Union County, North Carolina, USA

2nd Wife of Lewis Walter Broadaway

Name	Laura Hasty Winfield Broadaway
Gender	Female
Race	Colored (Black)
Age	50
Birth Year	ABT 1879
Marriage Date	4 Dec 1929
Marriage Place	Union, North Carolina, USA
Father	Henry Hasty
Mother	Emeline Hasty
Spouse	Lewis Broadaway
Spouse Gender	Male
Spouse Race	Colored (Black)
Spouse Age	62
Spouse Father	Hamp Broadaway
Spouse Mother	Cella Broadaway
Event Type	Marriage

Clayton Broadaway Sr 1904–1986

When Clayton Broadaway was born on January 15, 1904, in Burnsville, Anson, North Carolina, his father, Lewis, was forty and his mother, Edith, was thirty-eight. He married Kattie L Lotharp in 1924 in his hometown. They had fifteen children in twenty-seven years. He died on March 31, 1986, in Polkton, Anson, North Carolina, at the age of eighty-two, and was buried there.

Parents:
Lewis Walter Broadway 1863–1950
Edith Davis 1865–1928

Spouse:
Kattie L Lotharp 1911–1962
Children:
Annie Lee Broadway 1926–
Hattie Edith Broadway 1926–2011
Mary Lee Broadway 1928–2009
Johnnie Lewis Broadway 1930–1993
Minnie Leola Broadway 1932–2002
Evelyn Broadway 1933–1997
Eleanor Lucille Broadway 1935–
Flossie Broadway 1935–
Roosevelt Broadway 1938–2012
Samuel Earl Broadway 1940–
Geraldine Broadway 1943–
Katie Frances Broadway 1945–2009
Clayton Broadway Jr 1947–
John Truman Broadway 1949–2010
William "Bill" Broadway 1953–1953

Gaston Broadaway 1887-1924

When Gaston Broadway was born on February 28, 1887, in Burnsville, North Carolina, his father, Lewis, was twenty-three and his mother, Edith, was twenty-one. He married Bertha Turner on January 4, 1910, in Anson, North Carolina. They had eight children in seventeen years. He died on November 17, 1924, in his hometown at the age of thirty-seven, and was buried in China.

Parents:

Lewis Walter Broadway 1863–1950

Edith Davis 1865–1928

Spouse:

Bertha Turner 1893–1959

Children:

Edie Mae Broadway 1910–2009

Lola Vean Broadway 1912–2006

Louis Henry Broadway 1915–1971

Charlie Boyd Broadway 1917–1959

Kenneth Craig Broadaway 1919–1985

Edgienell Broadway 1921–2006

Gleen Broadway 1924–1924

Estella Broadway 1928–1994

family
is a gift that lasts
forever

SECTION VII JAMES BROADAWAY

Broadway Family History Trivia: *The 1866 Civil Rights Act and the Fourteenth* *Amendment guaranteed that African Americans were eligible to purchase land. Black homesteaders* *like our ancestors Marshall and Slyvia Broadway used it to build new lives in which they owned the* *land they worked, provided for their families, and educated their children.*

When James A Baucom-Broadaway and his brother Harry were born in 1815 in Burnsville, North Carolina, their father, Cannis Broadaway, was twenty. He had one child with Harriet Miney Broadway, one child with Charlotte Morris, and two children with Margaret Broadway. He died on May 19, 1881, in Wadesboro, North Carolina, at the age of sixty-six, and was buried in Polkton, North Carolina.

1. Marshall Baucom-Broadaway1850-1926 (1910 name spelled Broadway) 1850-1926, 1860 Lilesville, 1870 Burnsville, 1880 Lanesboro, NC, 1900 Hampton, Lee, AR (Broadaway), 1910 Hampton, Lee, AR (Broadaway), 1920 Hampton, AR, age 65 (Broadaway); Flint, MI, 1926 Chicago, Cook, IL
2. Oliver Broadaway (Broadway) 1874-1950, Lanesboro, Anson, NC, Hampton & Moro, AR
3. Samuel Broadway 1901-1992, Hampton & Moro, AR, Chicago, IL
4. Daniel Broadway 1920-1999, Helena, Phillips, AR, Hampton, Lee, AR, Little Rock, AR, Michigan 1951 & Illinois
5. Eugene Broadway, Moro & Little Rock, AR, Atlanta, GA

1870 United States Federal Census			
		Age in 1870	55
		Birth Date	abt 1815
Name	Jun	Birthplace	North
Broadaway		Carolina	

Dwelling Number	74	
Home in 1870	Burnsville,	
Anson, NC		
Race	Black	
Gender	Male	
Post Office	Wadesboro	
Occupation	Farm	
Laborer		
Cannot Read	Yes	
Cannot Write	Yes	
Male Citizen Over 21	Yes	
Inferred Children	Marsha	
Broadaway		
Household members		
Name	Age	
Jun Broadaway	55	
Marsha Broadaway	17	
Magaret Broadaway	30	
Jane Broadaway	14	
Mack Broadaway	10	

1880 United States Federal Census

Name	James Broadaway
Age	60
Birth Date	Abt 1820
Birthplace	North Carolina

Marshall B Broadaway 1850-1926
BIRTH 19 NOV 1850 • Burnsville, Anson County, NC
DEATH 10 FEB 1926 • Chicago, Cook, IL

Home in 1880   Lanesboro, Anson, NC

Dwelling Number	348
Race	Mulatto
Gender	Male
Relation to Head of House	
	Father
Marital Status	Widower
Father's Birthplace	North Carolina
Mother's Birthplace	North Carolina
Occupation	Farm laborer
Neighbors	View others on page.

Household members

Name	Age
Jane Watson	25
James Broadaway	60

U.S., Find A Grave Index, 1700s-Current

Name	James A Baucum
Cemetery	Old Westview Cemetery
Burial or Cremation Place:	Wadesboro, Anson County, NC

When Marshall Baucom Broadway was born on November 19, 1850, in Anson, North Carolina, his father, James, was thirty-five and his mother, Charlotte, was thirty-five. He married Silvy Jane Clark on February 20, 1873, in Ansonville, North Carolina. They had nine children in twenty-three years. He died on February 10, 1926, in Chicago, Illinois, at the age of seventy-five, and was buried in Blue Island, Illinois.

Parents

James Baucum Broadway 1815–1881

Charlotte Morris 1819–

Spouse

Silvy Jane Clark 1856–1916

Children

John Washington Broadway 1872–1936

Oliver James Broadway 1874–1950

Mary F (Helen) Broadway 1876–1880

Annie Liaza Broadway 1878–1933

William Cannie Broadway 1886–1928

Julia "Lessie" Broadway 1888–1952

Morris James Broadway 1893–1955

Julius Broadway 1894–1966

Senior Broadway 1896–1956

Surnames Used: Broadaway and Broadway

James Broadaway/Marshall Baucom-Broadaway (Broadway/**John Broadaway**
(Broadway)/

James Broadaway/Marshall Baucom-Broadaway (Broadway)/**Oliver Broadaway**
(Broadway)/Samuel Broadway/Daniel Broadway/Eugene Broadway

James Broadaway/Marshall Baucom-Broadaway (Broadway)/Julius

James Broadaway/Marshall Baucom-Broadaway (Broadway)/Morris

James Broadaway/Marshall Baucom-Broadaway (Broadway)/William Cannie

James Broadaway/Marshall Baucom-Broadaway (Broadway)/Julia Lessie

James Broadaway/Marshall Baucom-Broadaway (Broadway)/Senior

James Broadaway/Marshall Baucom-Broadaway (Broadway)/Mary E.

Marshall and Sylvia Broadaway's 1873 Marriage Certificate

Most helpful document in the research of Marshall and Sylvia's family. Shown in the
Picture Section are names of parents and alive or dead for parents of Marshall and
Sylvia. The marriage certificate also showed that Marshall changed his name from
Baucom to Broadaway to align with his father.

1860 U.S. Federal Census - Slave Schedules	Gender	Male
	Race	Black

Age 6
Birth Date abt 1854
Residence Date 1860
Residence Place Lilesville and
Morven, Anson, North
Carolina, USA
Role Slave
Slave Owner Alfred Baucum
Household members
Gender Age
Female 41
Male 27
Female 10
Male 6

1920 United States Federal Census

Name Marckell Broadway
Age 65
Birth Year abt 1855
Birthplace North Carolina
Home in 1920 Hampton, Lee,
Arkansas
Street Springfield Road
House Number Farm
Residence Date 1920
Race Black
Gender Male
Relation to Head of House Head
Marital Status Widowed
Father's Birthplace North
Carolina
Mother's Birthplace North
Carolina
Able to Speak English Yes
Occupation Farmer
Industry General Farm
Employment Field Own
Account

Able to read Yes
Able to Write Yes
Neighbors View others on
page.
Household members
Name Age
Marckell Broadway 65
Marry L Broadway 20
Senie Broadway 22
Lula Broadway 21
Othiler Broadway 1

Cook County, Illinois Death Index, 1908-1988

Name Marshall Broadway
Death Date 10 Feb 1926
Death Place Cook, Illinois, USA
File Number 6004023

Illinois, Deaths, and Stillbirths Index, 1916-1947

Name Marshall Broadway
Birth Date abt 1861
Birthplace No Carolina
Death Date 10 Feb 1926
Death Place Chicago, Cook,
Illinois
Burial Date 13 Feb 1926
Cemetery Name Lincoln
Death Age 65
Occupation Laborer
Race Black
Marital Status W
Gender Male
Residence Chicago, Cook, IL
Spouse Name T... Broadway
FHL Film Number 1877730

U.S., Find A Grave Index, 1600s-Current

Name   Marshall Baucum Broadway
Birth Date   19 Nov 1850
Death Date   10 Feb 1926
Cemetery   Lincoln Cemetery
Burial or Cremation Place: Blue Island, Cook County, Illinois, United States of America
Has Bio?   N
Spouse   Silvia Jane Broadway
Children   Morris James Broadway; John W. Broadway; William Cannie Broadway
Senior Broadway; Oliver James Broadway

Jane Broadaway 1854 -

When Jane Broadway was born in February 1854 in Anson, North Carolina, her father, James, was thirty-nine, and her mother, Margaret, was fourteen. She had one son and one daughter with Benjamin Watson. She then married Levi Darden and they had one son together. She had three brothers.

Parents:

James A Baucom-Broadway 1815–1881
Margaret Broadway 1840–

Spouse and Children:

Levi Darden 1857–1914
        Sam Darden 1879–

Spouse and Children:

Benjamin Watson 1850–
        Benjamin Watson 1876–
        Nellie Watson 1878–

North Carolina, Marriage Records, 1741-2011

Name   Jane Watson
Gender   Female
Race   Colored
Age   23
Birth Year   abt 1856
Marriage Date   15 Nov 1879
Marriage Place   Wayne, North Carolina, USA
Mother Judy Watson
Spouse Levi Durden
Spouse Gender   Male

Spouse Race	Colored (Black)
Spouse Age	25
Spouse Father	Isaac Hobbs
Spouse Mother	Rachel Durden
Event Type	Marriage

Mack Broadaway 1859 –

When Mack Broadway was born in 1859 in Polkton, North Carolina, his father, James, was forty-four and his mother, Margaret, was nineteen. He had two sons and two daughters with Clara Watson. He was buried in Polkton, North Carolina.

Guardian father: James A Baucom-Broadway: 1815–1881
Biological mother: Margaret Broadway 1840–

Spouse: Alice Viney Teal 1859–1888

Spouse: Sarah Jane Tyson 1872–

Spouse: Clara Watson 1874–1936
Children:
Glennie Broadway 1894–
Daisy Broadway 1895–
Wm Perlie Broadway 1899–
James Maxton Broadway 1899–1973

North Carolina, Marriage Records, 1741-2011

Name	Mack Broadaway
Gender	Male
Race	Colored (Black)
Age	22
Birth Year	abt 1859
Marriage Date	28 Jul 1881
Marriage Place	Anson, North Carolina, USA
Father	Jim Broadaway
Mother	Margaret Broadaway
Spouse	Vincy Teal
Spouse Gender	Female
Spouse Race	Colored (Black)
Spouse Age	23
Spouse Mother	Vincy Teal
Event Type	Marriage

Calvin Broadway 1840–1908

When Calvin Broadway was born in January 1840 in Burnsville, North Carolina, his father, James, was twenty-five and his mother, Harriet, was twenty-five. He married Narsica Anna Sturdivant, and they had fourteen children together. He then married Sallie Crawford on October 12, 1893, in Mecklenburg, North Carolina. He died in 1908 in Anson, North Carolina, at the age of sixty-eight.

Parents:

James A Baucom-Broadway 1815–1881
Harriet Miney Broadway 1815–1885

Spouse: Narsica Anna Sturdivant 1855–1935

Spouse: Sallie Crawford 1852–

Children:

1. Hattie J Broadway 1872–1946
2. Annie Baxter Broadway 1875–1930
3. Rachel Anna Broadway 1875–1930
4. Lula M Broadway 1876–1925
5. Lon Broadway 1879–1925
6. John Walter Broadway 1879–1959
7. Nannie Bell Broadway 1881–1956
8. Franklin P Broadway 1883–1946
9. Minnie V Broadway 1886–1943
10. Joseph Miller Broadway 1888–1962
11. Jesse Edward Broadway 1890–1964
12. Sidney Wilber "Walter" Broadway 1894–1936
13. Lonnie Clarence "LC" Broadway Sr 1897–1981
14. Narcis Broadway 1898–1963

family
is a gift that lasts
forever

SECTION VIII ROBERT "BOB" BROADAWAY

Broadaway Family History Trivia: Documented Slave Sale – January 4, 1836, Captain Frederick Staton sold Miney "Harriett" to John and Harriett Staton-Broadaway.

When Robert "Bob" Broadway and his twin brother Harry were born in 1817 in Ansonville, North Carolina, their father, Cannis Broadaway, was twenty-two. Robert married Harriet in Union County in 1853 and 1859. He then married Harriet Broadway on August 23, 1866. They had three children in thirteen years. He died in 1881 in Anson, North Carolina, at the age of sixty-four.

Spouse: Harriet M Broadway
> Harriet Miney Broadway was born in 1815 in Ansonville, North Carolina. She had one son with Daniel L Benton. She also had one son with James A Baucom-Broadway. She then married Robert "Bob" Broadway and they had three children together. She died in 1885 at the age of seventy.

Children of: Robert and Harriet M Broadway
- o George "Johnnie" Broadway 1842–1895
- o Lydia Broadway 1849–
- o Harriett Broadway 1855–

North Carolina Marriage Collection, 1741-2004			
Name	**Robert Broadaway**	Race	Black
		Spouse	Harriet Broadway
Gender	Male	Spouse Gender	Female
		Spouse Race	Black

Marriage Date   1853
Marriage County Union
Marriage State   North Carolina

North Carolina, Marriage Records, 1741-2011

Name   Robert Broadaway
Gender   Male
Race   Black
Marriage Date   1859
Marriage Place   Union, North
Carolina, USA
Spouse   Harriet Broadway
Spouse Gender   Female
Spouse Race   Black
Event Type   Marriage

North Carolina Marriage Collection, 1741-2004

Name   Robert Broadaway
Gender   Male
Spouse   Harriet Broadaway
Spouse Gender   Female
Marriage Date   23 Aug 1866
Marriage County Union
Marriage State   North Carolina
Source Record of this marriage may
be found at the Family

1880 United States Federal Census
Name   Robt. Broadaway
Age   63
Birth Date   Abt 1817
Birthplace   North Carolina
Home in 1880   Ansonville, Anson,
North Carolina, USA
Dwelling Number 64
Race   Black

1870 United States Federal Census
Name   Robert Broadway
Age in 1870   37
Birth Date   abt 1833
Birthplace   North Carolina
Dwelling Number   279
Home in 1870   Ansonville, Anson,
North Carolina
Race   White
Gender   Male
Post Office   Wadesboro
Occupation   Works on Railroad
Cannot Read   Yes
Cannot Write   Yes
Male Citizen Over 21   Yes
Household members

Name	Age
Robert Broadway	37
Works on Railroad	
Harriett Broadway	60
Keeps House	
Lydia Broadway	21
Ellen Broadway	4
Grandchild	
Harriet Broadway	15

Gender Male
Relation to Head of House Self
(Head)
Marital Status   Married
Spouse's Name   Harriett Broadaway
Father's Birthplace   North
Carolina
Mother's Birthplace   North
Carolina

56

Occupation   Laborer

Sick   Gravel

Cannot Read   Y

Cannot Write   Y

Neighbors   View others on page.

Household members

Name   Age

Robt. Broadaway   63
          Laborer - Gravel

Harriett Broadaway   75
          Wife

Ellen Broadaway   14
          Grandchild

North Carolina, Marriage Records, 1741-2011

Name   Bob Broadaway

Gender Male

Race   Colored (Black)

Age   67

Birth Year   abt 1817

Marriage Date   30 Dec 1884

Marriage Place   Anson, North Carolina, USA

Spouse   Mallie Gonld

Spouse Gender   Female

Spouse Race   Colored (Black)

Spouse Age   49

Event Type   Marriage

George "Johnnie" Broadway 1842-1895

When George "Johnnie" Broadway was born in 1842 in Clarendon, South Carolina, his father, Robert, was twenty-five and his mother, Harriet, was twenty-seven. He married Nancy Green in 1871 in Leon, Texas. They had nine children in fourteen years. He died in 1895 in Leon, Texas, at the age of fifty-three.

Parents: Robert "Bob" Broadway 1817–1881 and Harriet Miney Broadway 1815–1885

Spouse: Nancy Green 1855–1921

Children:

Fannie Broadway 1872–1940

Tiny Broadway 1873–1955

Ben Broadway 1878–1948

George Broadway Jr 1878–1958

Emma Whaley Broadway 1880–1969

John R Broadway Sr 1882–1955

Lethe Broadway 1882–1940

Lemon Broadway 1885–1948

Nannie Broadway 1886–1973

George Broadaway Jr. 1878-1958

When George Broadway was born on November 18, 1878, in Texas, his father, George, was thirty-six and his mother, Nancy, was twenty-three. He had four sons with Hattie E. Williams between 1895 and 1908. He died on March 1, 1958, in Houston, Texas, at the age of seventy-nine.

Parents: George "Johnnie" Broadway 1842–1895 and Nancy Green 1855–1921

Spouse: Hattie E. Williams 1892–1950

Children:
Horace Broadway 1895–1962
John Broadway 1902–
Jesse Broadway 1904–
Edell Broadway 1908–1964

Edell Broadway 1908-1964

When Edell Broadway was born on May 8, 1908, in Dallas, Texas, his father, George, was twenty-nine and his mother, Hattie, was sixteen. He had one son and three daughters with Ola Lagnone between 1929 and 1939. He died on July 7, 1964, in his hometown at the age of fifty-six, and was buried there.

Parents: George Broadway Jr 1878–1958 and Hattie E. Williams 1892–1950

Spouse: Ola Lagnone 1929–1992

Children:
Beatrice Broadway 1929–1992
Lorraine Broadway 1932–2004
Richard Broadway 1937–1970
Ethel Broadway 1939–

Lydia Broadaway

BIRTH 1849 • Ansonville, Anson County, North Carolina
DEATH Unknown

When Lydia Broadway was born in 1849 in Ansonville, North Carolina, her father, Robert, was 32, and her mother, Harriet, was 34. She married Sam Watson on January

26, 1871, in Anson, North Carolina. They had one child during their marriage. She had two brothers and one sister.

Parents
Robert "Bob" Broadway 1817–1881
Harriet Miney Broadway 1815–1885

Spouse
Sam Watson 1845–
Child
Ellen Broadway 1866–

1870 United States Federal Census

Name	Lydia Broadway	
Age in 1870	21	
Birth Date	abt 1849	
Birthplace	North Carolina	
Dwelling Number	279	
Home in 1870	Ansonville, Anson, North Carolina	
Race	Black	
Gender	Female	
Post Office	Wadesboro	
Occupation	No Occupation	
Cannot Read	Yes	
Cannot Write	Yes	
Household members		
Name	Age	

Robert Broadway 37
Harriett Broadway 60
Lydia Broadway 21
Ellen Broadway 4
Harriet Broadway 15

North Carolina, Marriage Records, 1741-2011

Name	Lycia Broadaway
Gender	Female
Marriage Date	26 Jan 1871
Marriage Place	Anson, NC
Spouse	Sam Watson
Spouse Gender	Male
Event Type	Marriage

Harriett Broadaway 1855-

When Harriett Broadway was born in 1855 in Ansonville, North Carolina, her father, Robert, was 38, and her mother, Harriet, was 40. She lived in Ansonville, North Carolina, in 1870. She had two brothers and one sister.

1870 United States Federal Census

Name	Harriet Broadway	Birthplace	North Carolina
Age in 1870	15	Dwelling Number	279
Birth Date	abt 1855	Home in 1870	Ansonville, Anson, NC

Race   Black
Gender Female
Post Office   Wadesboro
Occupation   No Occupation
Cannot Read   Yes
Cannot Write   Yes
Household members

Name	Age
Robert Broadway	37
Harriett Broadway	60
Lydia Broadway	21
Ellen Broadway	4
Harriet Broadway	**15**

SECTION IX HARRIETT "MINEY" BROADAWAY

Broadaway Family History Trivia: Affectionately, known as Miney, Harriett Broadaway experienced the sale of her person in 1836. Over thirty years later, in 1866 the 13th Amendment abolished slavery.

Harriet Miney Broadway was born in 1815 in Ansonville, North Carolina, a former slave. She had one son with Daniel L Benton. She also had one son with James A Baucom-Broadway. She then married Robert "Bob" Broadway and they had three children together. She died in 1885 at the age of seventy.

1836 Slave Sale: Miney Staton was sold to John & Harriett Broadaway (Became Miney "Harriett) Broadaway) – January 4, 1836. She was previously owned by Frederick Staton.

Parents: Slave Staton

Friends: Robert "Bob" Broadway 1817–1881
Children:
- George "Johnnie" Broadway 1842–1895
- Lydia Broadway 1849–
- Harriett Broadway 1855–

Friend: James A Baucom-Broadway 1815–1881
Children: Calvin Broadway 1840–1908

Friend: Daniel L Benton 1805–1893

Children: Sidney B. Broadway 1835–1923

1870 United States Federal Census

Name	Harriett Broadway
Age in 1870	60
Birth Date	abt 1810
Birthplace	North Carolina
Dwelling Number	279
Home in 1870	Ansonville, Anson, North Carolina
Race	Black
Gender	Female
Post Office	Wadesboro
Occupation	Keeping House
Cannot Read	Yes
Cannot Write	Yes

Household members

Name	Age
Robert Broadway	37
Harriett Broadway	60
Lydia Broadway	21
Ellen Broadway	4
Harriet Broadway	15

Spouse's Name	Robt. Broadaway
Father's Birthplace	North Carolina
Mother's Birthplace	North Carolina
Cannot Read	Y
Cannot Write	Y
Neighbors	View others on page.

Household members

Name	Age
Robt. Broadaway	63
Harriett Broadaway	75
Ellen Broadaway	14

1880 United States Federal Census

Name	Harriett Broadaway
Age	75
Birth Date	Abt 1805
Birthplace	North Carolina
Home in 1880	Ansonville, Anson, North Carolina, USA
Dwelling Number	64
Race	Black
Gender	Female
Relation to Head of House:	Wife
Marital Status	Married

Sidney B. Broadway 1835–1923

When Sidney B. Broadway was born in 1835 in Polkton, Anson, North Carolina, his father, Daniel, was thirty and his mother, Harriet, was twenty. He had three sons and two daughters with Mary Elizabeth Ledbetter. He also had one son with Cora Elizabeth Little. He then married Ella Jane Tyson and they had seven children together. He died on October 12, 1923, in West Southern Pines, Moore, North Carolina, having lived a long life of eighty-eight years.

Parents:
1847–1928
Daniel L Benton 1805–1893
Harriet Miney Broadway 1815–1885

Spouse: Ella Jane Tyson 1862–1949

Children:
Emma Tyson 1881–
Sidney Randal Broadway 1889–1928
Amos James Broadway 1893–1940
1847–
Gracie E Broadway 1895–1924
Charles Forester Broadway 1898–1983
Ellwood Broadway 1902–1936
1947–
Oscar William Broadway 1906–1954

Spouse: Mary Elizabeth Ledbetter

Children:
Ellen Broadway 1864–
John Broadway 1867–1946
Rae Broadway 1871–1947
Cannie Broadway 1873–1936
Cora Anna Broadway 1879–1933

Spouse: Cora Elizabeth Little

Children:
Norfolk Monroe Broadway 1871–

North Carolina Death Certificate: Sidney Broadway
Death: October 29, 1922
Husband of Ella J. Broadway
Informant was son, Sidney Broadway
Name of Father: Cannis B of Polkton; Mother: unknown
Farmer in Polkton, Anson, NC

North Carolina, U.S., Newspapers.com™ Stories and Events Index, 1800s-current
Name	Sidney Broadaway
Residence Date	7 Dec 1882
Residence Place	Wadesboro, North Carolina, USA
Newspaper Title	The Anson Times

U.S., Confederate Army Payrolls for Enslaved Labor, 1840-1883
Name	Jno Broadaway
Role	Enslaver

Business Name   Dist Cape Fear
Payroll Number   1988
Enslaved PersonSidney; George

North Carolina, Deaths, 1906-1930
Name   Sidney B. Broadway
Birthplace   Polkton, NC
Spouse   Ella J. Tyson
Children   Sidney Randal Broadway

John Broadway 1867–1946

When John Broadway was born on February 14, 1867, in Lanesboro, Anson, North Carolina, his father, Sidney, was thirty-two and his mother, Mary, was twenty. He married Ann Eliza Davis on December 13, 1888, in Anson, North Carolina. They had twelve children in twenty-two years. He died on January 5, 1946, in Lumberton, Robeson, North Carolina, at the age of seventy-eight, and was buried there.

Parents:
  Sidney B. Broadway 1835–1923
  Mary Elizabeth Ledbetter 1847–1928
Spouse:
  Unknown
  Ann Eliza Davis 1873–
Children:
  Rosa Broadway 1891–1913
  Cannie Broadway 1895–1943
  Josie Broadway 1896–
  Lilla Broadway 1897–1927
  Thitus Broadway 1900–
  Mary Jane Broadway 1901–1994
  Flonnie L. Broadway 1903–1927
  Inez B. Broadway 1906–
  John "Willie" Broadway 1906–
  Chester Broadway 1909–
  Craig Broadway Sr 1910–1995
  Hattie Mae Broadway 1914–2000

Hattie Mae Broadway 1914–2000

When Hattie Mae Broadway was born on March 30, 1914, in Anson, North Carolina, her father, John, was forty-seven, and her mother, Ann, was forty-one. She had three children with Willie Lee Jones and one child with Thomas J Sturdivant. She died on

November 7, 2000, in Winston-Salem, Forsyth, North Carolina, at the age of eighty-six, and was buried there.

Parents:
John Broadway 1867–1946
2006
Ann Eliza Davis 1873–

Spouse: Thomas J Sturdivant 1915–
Children: Willie Mae Broadway 1932–

Spouse: Willie Lee Jones 1914–
Children: Curtis Jones 1932–
              Leonder Jones 1939–
              Essie Mae Jones –1937

Social Security Death Index
Name   Hattie M. Broadway
Social Security Number   244-30-8969
Birth Date   30 Mar 1914
Issue year   Before 1951
Issue State   North Carolina
Last Residence   27101, Winston Salem, Forsyth, North Carolina, USA
Death Date   1 Nov 2000

U.S. WWII Draft Cards Young Men, 1898-1929
Name   Mrs. Hattie J Jones
Gender   Female
Relationship to Draftee Wife
Residence Place   Red Springs, Robeson, North Carolina, USA
Registration Date   1940
Registration Place   Red Springs, Robeson
Household members
Name   Relationship
Willie Lee Jones   Self (Head)
Hattie J Jones   Wife

U.S., Social Security Applications and Claims Index, 1936-2007
Name   Hattie M Broadway
Gender Female
Spouse Thomas Sturidivant
Child   Willie Mae Broadway

Virginia, Marriage Records, 1936-2014

Name   Hattie McBride (maiden name)
Gender Female
Spouse Willie Lee Jones
Child   Curtis Jones
Certificate Number   1951036928

Web: Obituary Daily Times Index, 1995-2012

Name   Hattie Mae Broadway
Age   86
Birth Date   Abt 1914
Death Date   abt 2000
Death Place   Winston-Salem NC
Publication Date 12 Nov 2000
Publication Place USA
Tombstone   0

Willie Mae Broadway 1932–2006

When Willie Mae Broadway was born on September 15, 1932, in Ansonville, Anson, North Carolina, her father, Thomas, was seventeen, and her mother, Hattie, was eighteen. She had three children with B. Jones and three other children. She died on September 22, 2006, in Winston-Salem, Forsyth, North Carolina, at the age of seventy-four.

Parents:
Thomas J Sturdivant 1915–
Hattie Mae Broadway 1914–2000

Spouse:
B Jones
Children:
Robert Lee Jones
Howard Jones
Ray Jones –2017

Children:
Angela Marie Broadway 1955–2009
Francina M Broadway
Ernest H Broadway

Social Security Death Index

Name	Willie M. Jones
Social Security Number	246-46-4789
Birth Date	15 Sep 1932
Issue year	Before 1951
Issue State	North Carolina
Last Residence	27105, Winston Salem, Forsyth, North Carolina
Death Date	22 Sep 2006

Web: Obituary Daily Times Index, 1995-2012

Name	Willie Mae Jones
Age	71
Birth Date	Abt 1935
Death Date	abt 2006
Death Place	Winston-Salem NC
Publication Date	27 Sep 2006
Publication Place	USA
Tombstone	0

Francina M Broadaway

When Francina M Broadaway was born in Winston-Salem, North Carolina, her mother, Willie, was twenty-nine. She has two children with Tony Hairston and two other children. She had five siblings.

Mother: Willie Mae Broadway 1932–2006
Spouse: Tony Hairston 1957–
Children:
1. Anthony Broadaway
2. Marquita Broadaway
3. Jonta Broadaway
4. Leshaun Trey Broadaway

Anthony Broadaway

When Anthony Broadaway was born in Winston-Salem, North Carolina, his father, Tony, was twenty-nine and his mother, Francina, was twenty-five. He lived in Winston-Salem, North Carolina, for more than two years from 1993 to 1995. He has two brothers and one sister.

Marquita Broadaway

When Marquita Broadaway was born in Winston-Salem, North Carolina, her father, Tony, was thirty, and her mother, Francina, was twenty-six. She has three brothers.

SECTION X GEORGE BROADAWAY

Broadway Family History Trivia: *Broadaway Ancestor George was born in 1835. Some thirty years later, in 1867 the 14th amendment grants African Americans birthright citizenship.*

George Broadway was born in 1835 in Lanesboro, North Carolina. He had one child with Phylis Parker and six children with Harriet Broadway. He lived in Lanesboro, North Carolina, in 1870 and moved to Ansonville, North Carolina, sometime between 1870 and 1880.

Parents: Unknown

Spouse: Phylis Parker 1840- ; Lanesboro Township, Anson, NC
Phylis Parker was born in 1840 in North Carolina. She had one son with George Broadway in 1859.
Child:

George W Maske 1859-1928
When George Wesly Maske was born in March 1859 in Ansonville, North Carolina, his father, George, was 24 and his mother, Phylis, was 19. He married Mary Thomas, and they had 14 children together. He then married Octavio Carter on October 3, 1914, in Halifax, North Carolina. He died on May 9, 1928, in Hamlet, North Carolina, at the age of 69, and was buried there.

Spouse: Harriet Broadaway 1848-1923
Harriet Broadway was born in 1848 in Lanesboro, North Carolina. She had four sons and two daughters with George Broadway between 1868 and 1879. She moved 3 times during her lifetime. She lived in Lanesboro, North Carolina, in 1870 and 1880,

then moved to Memphis, Tennessee by 1891. She died on November 24, 1923, in Kings, New York, having lived a long life of seventy-five years.

Children:
1. Jenia Broadaway 1868
2. Bose Broadaway, 1871
3. James E Broadaway 1874-1940
4. Dave Broadaway, 1878-1914
5. Watt Broadaway 1878
6. Charlotte C. Broadaway 1879

1870 United States Federal Census

Name   Harriet Broadaway
Birthplace   North Carolina
Dwelling Number 274
Home in 1870   Lanesboro, Anson, North Carolina
Race   Black
Gender   Female
Post Office   Wadesboro
Occupation   Keeping House
Cannot Read   Yes
Cannot Write   Yes
Inferred Spouse George Broadaway
Household members
Name   Age
George Broadaway   35
Harriet Broadaway   20
Info: Sydney, Elizabeth, and John Broadaway were neighbors of George and Harriett, 1870, Lanesboro, NC

1880 United States Federal Census

Name   Hariett Broadaway
Age   32
Birth Date   Abt 1848
Birthplace   North Carolina
Home in 1880   Ansonville, Anson, North Carolina, USA
Dwelling Number   101
Race   Black
Gender   Female
Relation to Head of House - Wife
Marital Status Married
Spouse's Name   George Broadaway
Father's Birthplace   North Carolina

Mother's Birthplace   North
Carolina
Occupation   Housekeeper
Cannot Read   Y
Cannot Write   Y
Neighbors   View others on
page.
Household members

Name	Age
George Broadaway	46
Hariett Broadaway	32
Jenia Broadaway	12
Bose Broadaway	9
Jim Broadaway	6
Watt Broadaway	2
Charlotte C. Broadaway	5/12

Info: Down the road from George
was H Broadaway 65
Eliza 54 wife, Julius 17 son, Puss 11
daughter, Henry 14 grandson, Flake
Annie 3 daughter

Tennessee, Death Records, 1908-1958

Name	Harriett Broadway
Gender	Female
Birthplace	USA
Spouse	George Broadway
Child	Dave Broadway
Certificate Number	77

North Carolina Slave Church Record 1857-1863
Negro Church Roll

Slave Owner, John Broadaway listed Negroes who belonged to him: Harry, Bob, Sidney

U.S., Confederate Army Payrolls for Enslaved Labor, 1840-1883

Name	Jno Broadaway
Role	Enslaver
Business Name	Dist Cape Fear
Payroll Number	1988
Enslaved Persons	Sidney; George

family
is a gift that lasts
forever

SECTION XI PICTURE & DOCUMENT GALLERY

SLAVE OWNERS – REV. JOHN BROADAWAY AND HARRIETT STATON BROADAWAY

Slave Sale of Miney Staton

Slave Sale - January 4, 1836
Anson County NC Deed Book Z page 357

Frederick Staton to John Broadaway & wife.

Received of John Broadaway Jr. and Harriett Broadaway his wife Five hundred fifty dollars in full payment of a ? negro woman by the name, of miney about thirty one, more of sale for which negro I warrant and forever defend the right and title from all other claims. I further relinquish my self & assign the ? 4th Jan. 1836.

Test: Uriah Staton . Frederick B Staton (Seal)

more ? June ?1837. That this Bill of sale was duly proven in open court by ?

ordered to be Registered. ? N. D. Boggan Clk.

Slave Owner, Frederick Staton Photo
Slave Owner, Frederick Staton Photo
Capt Frederick Staton

Birth: 1772
          Tarboro
          Edgecombe County
          North Carolina, USA
Death: Jan. 29, 1864
          Burnsville
          Anson County
          North Carolina, USA

Frederick Staton was a Captain in the War of
1812. Originally from Tarboro, NC he became a
large land owner in NW Anson County of over
5,000 acres. Much of this land passed out of
the family following the civil war. Most of the
Statons of Western North Carolina, numbering
in the thousands, are descendants of Frederick
Staton.

Family links:
 Spouses:
  Rhoda *Shannon* Staton*
  Priscilla *Corbin* Staton (1766 - 1854)*
  Sally *Tomlinson* Staton (1780 - 1859)*

 Children:
  Ennis Staton (1798 - 1885)*
  Uriah Staton (1807 - 1879)*
  Maniza *Staton* Staton (1812 - 1864)*

Added by: James Mason Fritz

DOCUMENTED SLAVES OF REV. JOHN BROADAWAY: JOHN, SYDNEY, HARRY, GEORGE. JAMES AND MARSHALL IN CHURCH ROLL 1857 – 1863

CHURCH ROLL 1857 - 1863
(Negro)

Moses	Belonging to Mrs. Moore	Sidney	Belonging to John Broadaway By baptism 1857
Ben	Belonging to R. Ricketts		
Jinkens	Belonging to E. B. Simmons	Ester	Belonging to John Sturdivant
Harry	Belonging to John Broadaway	Armeca	Belonging to Joseph Burch
Bob	Belonging to Walter Jones	Lucy	Belonging to Joseph Burch
Caleb	Belonging to Dr. Myers Granted Letter Oct., 1857	Smithy	Belonging to John Green
		Tillon	Belonging to Mrs. Moore
Bob	Belonging to John Broadaway	Lucy	Belonging to R. Ricketts
Clem	Belonging to W. F. Kendall	Winey	Belonging to J. R. Wood
Arch	Belonging to W. H. Benton	Hody	Belonging to John Cochran
Bill	Belonging to T. A. Thomas	Clary	Belonging to James E. Wood
Bertha	Belonging to Mrs. Leak	Forbis	Belonging to James Carraway
Araby	Belonging to Sarah E. Flake By baptism 1857	Ann	Belonging to Noval Bennett
		Tillar	Belonging to M. T. Picketts
Mary	Belonging to Jesse Liles	Roxy	Belonging to Joel McLendon
Lucy	Belonging to Jesse Liles	Rachel	Belonging to John McLendon

MARSHALL BAUCOM BROADAWAY AND SLYVIA CLARK MARRIAGE LICENSE

The State of North Carolina,

No.

COUNTY.

To any ordained Minister of any Religious Denomination, or to any Justice of the Peace, for said county. _____ having applied to me for a license for the marriage of *Marshall Baucom*, of *Lanstro*, aged *22* years, color *col*, son of *Jas Broadaway*, and *Charlotte Morris* and *is living* *is dead*, and reside at *Lanstro*, in the State of _____ and *Silvy Clark*, aged *14* years, color *col*, daughter of *Same Ingram*, and *Hannah Clark* and *is living* *is living*, and reside at _____, in the State of _____

family is a gift that lasts forever

1840-1883 CONFEDERATE ARMY PAYROLLS FOR ENSLAVED LABOR FOR REV. JOHN BROADAWAY SLAVES: SYDNEY AND GEORGE BROADAWAY

SLAVE OWNERS' HEADSTONES: STATON, BROADAWAY, BAUCON, BAUCUM, MORRIS FAMILIES

Aunt Margaret Winfield, who quietly bossed "Her Hill," and well-raised many useful daughters.

family
is a gift that lasts
forever

PARTIAL ARTICLE ON REV. JOHN BROADAWAY: Headstone of Rev. John Broadaway; Churches that allowed slaves to belong; John Broadaway's Plantation Site that Eugene, Jerome, and Marie researched and visited.

River Baptist Church   83

minutes:

Rev. John Broadaway is mentioned here as a preacher for the first and only time. He was a good man of considerable means but was probably only a licensed preacher. He married a sister of Uriah Staton.

Colored members bore only given names and were designated as belonging to certain masters.

Meetings then did not last long, usually closing on Tuesday or Wednesday after the opening Sabbath.

Sunday, as we call it, was never spoken of other than as the Lord's Day or Sabbath. It sounds well yet.

Jan. 1849. Samuel P. Morton presents his letter from Ebenezer, Stanly County. It was dated December, 1848. This is still on file and unsoiled.

This was an unfruitful year. Bro. Uriah Staton's Mariah the only addition during the year.

Thank God! Yes! We found the plantation site where Grandpa James and Grandpa Marshall lived in 1880.

family
is a gift that lasts
forever

War of 1812 Service Records

Name   Jesse Broadaway

Company   DAVIS' BATTALION, WEST TENNESSEE MILITIA.

Rank - Induction   PRIVATE

Rank - Discharge   PRIVATE

North Carolina Marriage Bonds, 1741-1868

Name   Jesse Broadaway

Gender   Male

Spouse   Unity Serratt

Spouse Gender Female

Bond date   10 Dec 1799

Bond #   000106788

Marriage Date 19 Dec 1858

Level Info   North Carolina Marriage Bonds, 1741-1868

Bondsman   John Brodaway

Witness   William Hicks

Performed By   James King

1860 U.S. Federal Census - Slave Schedules

Name   Wm Broadaway

Residence Date   1860

Residence Place   Meltonsville, Anson, NC

Number of Enslaved People   14

Role Slave Owner

Gender	Age
Female	38, 37
Male	21, 20, 16, 14, 12
Female	12
Male	9, 9, 8
Female	6, 4
Male	2

1860 United States Federal Census

Name   William Broadaway

Age   55

Birth Year   abt 1805

Gender   Male

Race   White

Birthplace   North Carolina
Home in 1860   Meltonsville, Anson, NC
Post Office   White Store
Occupation   Farmer
Real Estate Value   1500
Personal Estate Value 15000
Inferred Spouse   S A Broadaway
Inferred Child   J T Broadaway

Name	Age
William Broadaway	55
S A Broadaway	35
J T Broadaway	1
W L Broadaway	9
C C Broadaway	6
S E Broadaway	8
J Broadaway	4
H Broadaway	2
E E Broadaway	3/12

American Civil War Soldiers
Name   William Broadaway
Residence   Anson County, NC
Occupation   Artist
Enlistment Date   22 May 1861
Enlistment Place   Anson County, NC
Side Served   Confederacy
State Served   North Carolina

1870 United States Federal Census
Name   William Broadaway
Age in 1870 65
Birth Date   abt 1805
Birthplace   North Carolina
Home in 1870   White Store, Anson, NC
Race   White
Gender   Male
Post Office   Wadesboro
Occupation   Farmer
Personal Estate Value 600
Real Estate Value   1900

Inferred Spouse   Sarah Broadaway
Inferred Children   Walter L Broadaway
Name   Age
William Broadaway   65
Sarah Broadaway   46
Walter L & Eugenia Broadaway 17
Christopher Broadaway 16
Isham Broadaway   13
Hellen Broadaway   11
Ella Broadaway   9
Mary Broadaway   7
Anah Broadaway   5
Francis Broadaway   2

family
is a gift that lasts
forever

John David King Broadway Family

John D. King, John D., Wriston Cane, Phyllis, Margaret Gwen, Wilma Virginia Broadaway

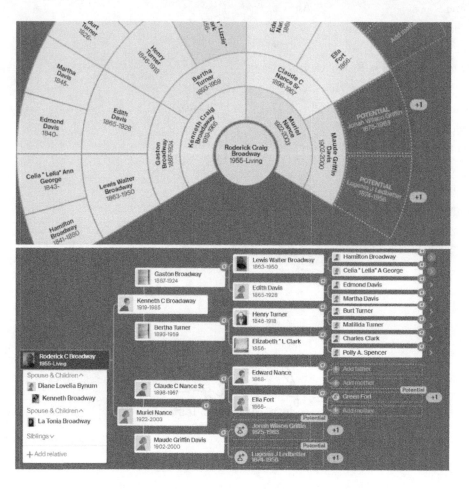

JOE FRED BROADAWAY
Row 3: Mable Lindsey Broadaway, Ruby J. Tilman Broadaway, Tammy Broadaway

family
is a gift that lasts
forever

CREASIE BROADAWAY 1827, Slave

Creasie Broadaway whereabouts from the NC Slave Schedule and U.S. Federal Census

Maiden Name: Creasie Broadaway
Married Name: Harriet "Creasie" Barrett

1848 Married: John Barrett

Six Barrett children
Four Broadaway children

1860 NC Slave Schedule

Gender	Female
Race	Black
Age	37
Birth Date	abt 1823
Residence Date	1860
Residence Place	Meltonsville, Anson, North Carolii
Role	Slave
Slave Owner	Wm Broadaway

Household members

Gender	Age
Female	38
Female	37
Male	21
Male	20
Male	16
Male	14
Male	12
Female	12
Male	9
Male	9
Male	8
Female	6
Female	4
Male	2

1880 U.S. Federal Census

Name	Creacy Broadaway
Age	54
Birth Date	Abt 1826
Birthplace	North Carolina
Home in 1880	Whites Store, Anson, North Carolina
Dwelling Number	91
Race	Black
Gender	Female
Marital Status	Widowed
Father's Birthplace	North Carolina
Mother's Birthplace	North Carolina
Occupation	House ...
Cannot Read	Y
Cannot Write	Y
Neighbors	View others on page

Household members

Name	Age
Creacy Broadaway	54

1870 U.S. Federal Census

Name	Creacy Braudaway
Age in 1870	43
Birth Date	abt 1827
Birthplace	North Carolina
Dwelling Number	242
Home in 1870	White Store, Anson, North Carolina
Race	Black
Gender	Female
Post Office	Wadesboro
Occupation	Keeping House
Cannot Read	Yes
Cannot Write	Yes

Household members

Name	Age
Aly Braudaway	
Creacy Braudaway	43

1900 U.S. Federal Census

Name	Harriet Barrett
Age	80
Birth Date	
Birthplace	North Carolina, USA
Home in 1900	Sandy Ridge, Union, North Carolina
Ward of City	4904
Sheet Number	5
Number of Dwelling in Order of Visitation	80
Family Number	81
Race	Black
Gender	Female
Relation to Head of House	Mother
Marital Status	Widowed
Father's Birthplace	North Carolina, USA
Mother's Birthplace	North Carolina, USA
Can Read	N
Can Write	N
Can Speak English	Y
Neighbors	View others on page

Household members

Name	Age
Harriet Barrett	80
Caroline Barrett	40
John C Barrett	14
Sis Barrett	5
Mamie Barrett	4

family
is a gift that lasts
forever

ALEXANDER BROADAWAY
1924 Death Certificate Alexander Broadaway Parents, Creasie Broadaway | John Barrett

Alexander Broadaway Family

MARSHALL C. BROADWAY
Bob Robert and Donnell Broadway

Bob "Robert" Broadway
Birth: January 5, 1874, Anson County, North Carolina
Death: 1920, Hampton, Lee County, Arkansas

Family
Father: Marshall Broadway, 1847-
Mother: Elizabeth Shavers 1847-1929

Spouse: Hattie L. Richardson 1879-
Children:
1. E Lizza Broadway, 1905-

Spouse: Bessie Beasley, 1896-
Children:
1. Ora L. Broadway, -1909-1990 (Spouse: Samuel O. Johnson)
2. Ruthie Cynthia Clark, 1912-
3. John S. Broadway, 1916-, (Spouse: Martha Harris 1909-1983; Children: John Broadway 1929-1983, Donnell Broadway 1934-2013 (Spouse: Annie L. Rogers))
4. Wesley Albert Broadway, 1920-1994, (Spouse: Willie Ben Wilson 1921-)
5. Ishman Broadway, 1921-1935

Donnell Broadway
Birth: October 9, 1934, Moro, Lee, Arkansas
Death: January 31, 2013, Marshall, Saline County, Missouri

Family
Father: John S. Broadway, 1916-
Mother: Martha Harris 1909-1937

Spouse: Ida F. Hodges 1935--
Children:
1. None listed.

Spouse: Mary Charlene VanBuren 1932-2006--
Children:
1. None listed.

Spouse: Savannah L. Thomas
Children:

1. David J. Broadway 1969-2014
2. Rochelle Broadway
3. Tamela Broadway
4. Cynthia Broadway

Spouse: Verna Mae Kimber 1937-
Children:
1. Mary Jane Kimber 1954-
   a. Alonzo Kimber
   b. Carma Evette Kimber

ORLANDER LANE BROADWAY
Sandy & Mary Clark, Arlander & Sarah Clark

Sandy Clark
1851-1925

Mary Clark
1851-1912

Arlander Broadway
1884-1949

Sarah Clark
1889-19??

family
is a gift that lasts
forever

DEATH CERTIFICATES of Arlander 1949 & Ellis 1948 Broadway, sons of Marshall C. Broadaway

ARKANSAS STATE BOARD OF HEALTH
CERTIFICATE OF DEATH
5485
Registration District No. 6038
Primary Registration District No.
STATE FILE NO.
1. PLACE OF DEATH a. COUNTY Lee
b. CITY OR TOWN Moro
c. LENGTH OF STAY 60
d. FULL NAME OF HOSPITAL OR INSTITUTION
2. USUAL RESIDENCE a. STATE Ark b. COUNTY Lee
c. CITY OR TOWN Moro
d. STREET ADDRESS
1949
3. NAME OF DECEASED (First) Arlander (Last) Broadway
4. DATE OF DEATH April 11 – 49
5. SEX Male
6. COLOR OR RACE Colored
7. MARRIED, NEVER MARRIED, WIDOWED, DIVORCED Married
8. DATE OF BIRTH Oct. 10
9. AGE 65
10a. USUAL OCCUPATION Farmer
10b. KIND OF BUSINESS OR INDUSTRY
11. BIRTHPLACE N. Carolina
12. CITIZEN OF WHAT COUNTRY? U.S.
13. FATHER'S NAME Marshall Broadway
14. MOTHER'S MAIDEN NAME Bettie
15. WAS DECEASED EVER IN U. S. ARMED FORCES? No
16. SOCIAL SECURITY NO.
17. INFORMANT Pearl Broadway 7948

CERTIFICATE OF DEATH
Registration District No.
Primary Registration District No.
STATE FILE NO.
PLACE OF DEATH
Lee
Hampton, Rural
LENGTH OF STAY 40yrs
none
2. USUAL RESIDENCE a. STATE Ark b. COUNTY Lee
c. CITY OR TOWN Rural Hampton
d. STREET ADDRESS Rt 2 Box 65, Moro, Ark.
FEB 17 1948
NAME Ellis Broadway
4. DATE OF DEATH January
6. COLOR OR RACE Colored
7. MARRIED, NEVER MARRIED, WIDOWED, DIVORCED Widow
8. DATE OF BIRTH May 1881
9. AGE 67
10b. KIND OF BUSINESS OR INDUSTRY Farm
11. BIRTHPLACE S. Caroline
13. FATHER'S NAME Marshall Broadway
14. MOTHER'S MAIDEN NAME Betty Broadway
16. SOCIAL SECURITY NO. None.
17. INFORMANT Mary Clark, Rt 2, Moro, Ark.
MEDICAL CERTIFICATION

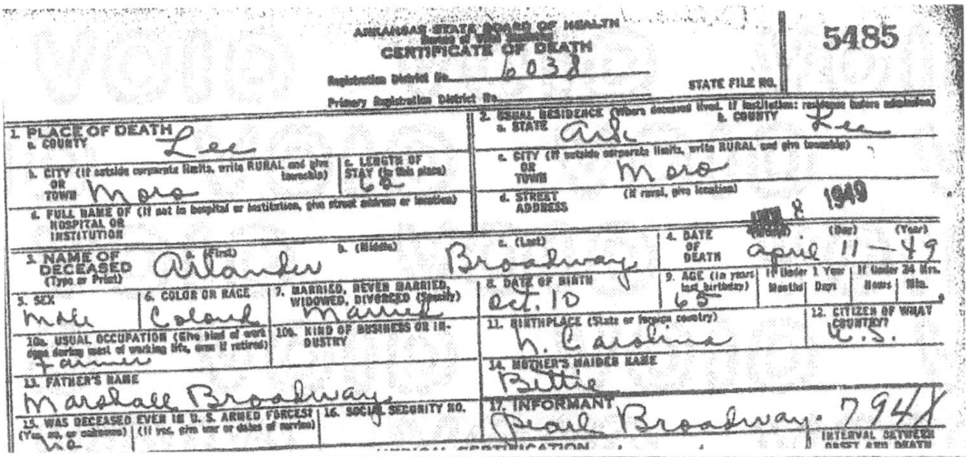

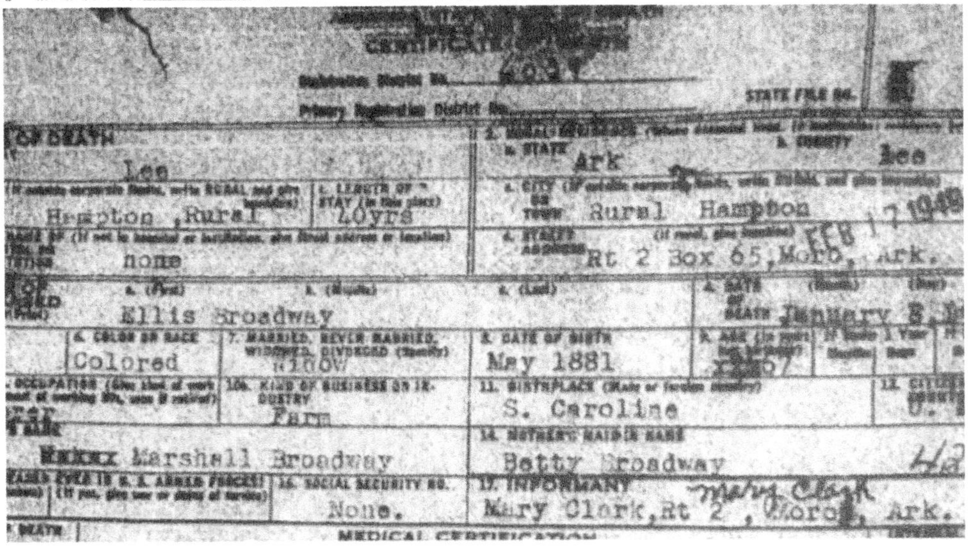

Arlander Broadway Family

family
is a gift that lasts
forever

Q.T. Broadway, his dad is Vernell Thomas Broadway

Dorthula Broadway-Jones

Minus Jones

Cuba Broadway

family
is a gift that lasts
forever

90

HARRY BROADAWAY

HARRY, BOB, AND SIDNEY WERE SLAVES 1857-1863

CHURCH ROLL 1857 - 1863

(Negro)

Moses	Belonging to Mrs. Moore	Sidney	Belonging to John Broadaway
Ben	Belonging to R. Ricketts		By baptism 1857
Jinkens	Belonging to H. B. Hammons	Ester	Belonging to John Sturdivant
Harry	Belonging to John Broadaway	Aneca	Belonging to Joseph Burch
Bob	Belonging to Walter Jones	Lucy	Belonging to Joseph Burch
Caleb	Belonging to Dr. Myers	Smithy	Belonging to John Grace
	Granted letter Oct., 1857	Tillon	Belonging to Mrs. Moore
Bob	Belonging to John Broadaway	Lucy	Belonging to R. Ricketts
Clem	Belonging to W. P. Kendall	Winny	Belonging to J. R. Wood
Arch	Belonging to W. H. Benton	Nody	Belonging to John Cochran
Bill	Belonging to T. A. Thomas	Clury	Belonging to James R. Wood
Martha	Belonging to Mrs. Leak	Forlum	Belonging to James Caraway
Anaky	Belonging to Sarah E. Flake	Ann	Belonging to Nevel Bennett
	By baptism 1857	Tillar	Belonging to M. I. Ricketts
Mary	Belonging to Jesse Idles	Rosy	Belonging to Joel McLendon
Lucy	Belonging to Jesse Idles	Rachel	Belonging to John McLendon

NORTH CAROLINA STATE BOARD OF HEALTH
BUREAU OF VITAL STATISTICS

STANDARD CERTIFICATE OF DEATH

1 PLACE OF DEATH
County _____ Registration District No. 63-5 540   Register No. 20
Township Machruil   State _____
City _____   or Village _____
No. _____ (If death occurred in a hospital or institution, give its NAME instead of street and number

2 FULL NAME Sidney Broadwa_

(a) Residence. No. _____ St. _____ Ward.
(Usual place of abode)   (If nonresident give city or town and State)
Length of residence in city or town where death occurred   yrs. _____ mos. _____ ds. _____ How long in U. S. if of foreign birth? yrs. _____ mos. _____ d_

PERSONAL AND STATISTICAL PARTICULARS	MEDICAL CERTIFICATE OF DEATH
3 Sex male	16 Date of Death (month, day, and year) Oct. 12 19 2.
4 Color or Race Colord	17
5 Single, Married, Widowed, or Divorced (write the word) married	I HEREBY CERTIFY, That I attended deceased fro_
5a If married, widowed, or divorced Husband of (or) Wife of Husband of Ella Broadway	Sept 12 , 1922 to Sept 29 , 19 2
6 Date of birth (month, day, and year)	that I last saw h__ alive on Sept 29 , 19 2
7 Age years Months Days If LESS than 1 day....hrs. about 79	and that death occurred, on the date stated above, at 3-4 A. The CAUSE OF DEATH was as follows:

family
is a gift that lasts
forever

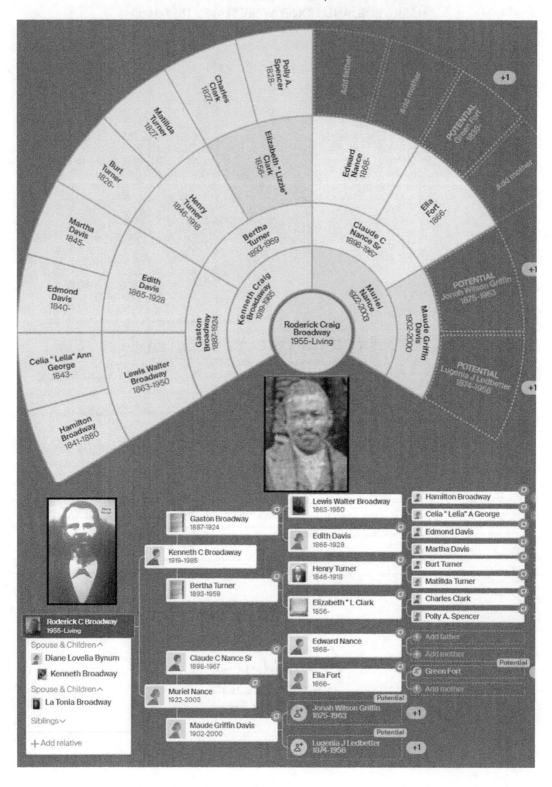

HAMILTON BROADAWAY FAMILY

LEWIS WALTER BROADAWAY FAMILY

GASTON BROADWAY FAMILY

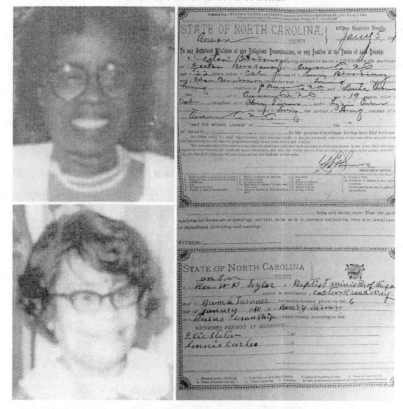

CLAYTON BROADAWAY

CLAYTON BROADAWAY FAMILY

CHARLES R. BROADAWAY

In Loving Memory
of
MR. CRAIG BROADAWAY

Tuesday, July 2, 1985 – 2:00 P.M.

ST. MATTHEWS UNITED CHURCH OF GOD
Oakboro, North Carolina

ELDER B. L. CURRY, *Pastor*

Order of Service

REV. J. N. COBLE, *Officiating*

MUSICAL PRELUDE.....................Mr. Albert Rush

PROCESSIONAL.......................Pianist

INVOCATION.........................Rev. J. N. Coble

HYMN...............................The Church Choir

SCRIPTURES:
OLD TESTAMENT.......................Psalm 23
NEW TESTAMENT.......................I Corin. 13

PRAYER OF COMFORT.................Rev. L. T. Willoughby

Obituary

MR. CRAIG BROADWAY departed this life Friday, June 28, 1985 in the Veterans Administration Medical Center, Salisbury, North Carolina following a lengthy illness. The son of the late Bertha and Caston Broadway, he was born in Anson County, North Carolina, reared in Stanly County and educated in the public schools of Stanly County.

He was a World War II Veteran and was a member of the Masonic Lodge Number 147. He attended the St. Matthews Church of God and was employed by the W. F. Briskley Construction Company, before his illness.

He will be greatly missed by his loving family and friends.

He is survived by his devoted wife, Mrs. Muriel Nance Broadway, of the home; one son, Roderick Craig Broadway of Durham, North Carolina; four daughters, Mrs. Pamelia Monroe of Oakboro, North Carolina, Ms. Priscilla Broadway of Charlotte, North Carolina, Mrs. Norma Boseman of Winston-Salem, North Carolina and Mrs. Bonnie Smith of Stuttgart, Germany; four sisters, Mrs. Edith Townsend of Greensboro, North Carolina, Mrs. L. V. Smith, Mrs. Edgie Nell Bivens and Mrs. Estella Ridenhour all of Oakboro, North Carolina; one uncle, Clayton Broadway of Burnsville, North Carolina; ten grandchildren; three aunts, Mrs. Minnie Thomas of Wadesboro, N.C., Mrs. Ella Nedley and Mrs. Ida Lothorp both of Washington, D.C.; one daughter-in-law, Mrs. Diane Byrum Broadway; two sons-in-law, Dr. Charles T. Smith and Rev. Alexander Boseman; a number of nieces, nephews, other relatives and friends, including other in-laws.

PALLBEARERS
Masons

FLOWER BEARERS
Cousins

* * * * * *

"THE CLOCK OF LIFE"

The clock of life is wound but once,
And no man has the power to tell
Just when the hands will stop,
At late or early hour.

To lose one's wealth is sad indeed
To lose one's health is more

GILES, HARRY AND ELIZA BROADAWAY FAMILY

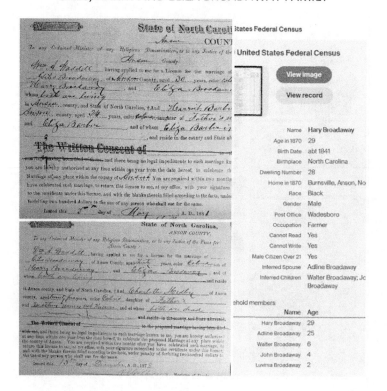

States Federal Census

United States Federal Census

Name	Hary Broadaway
Age in 1870	29
Birth Date	abt 1841
Birthplace	North Carolina
Dwelling Number	28
Home in 1870	Burnsville, Anson, No
Race	Black
Gender	Male
Post Office	Wadesboro
Occupation	Farmer
Cannot Read	Yes
Cannot Write	Yes
Male Citizen Over 21	Yes
Inferred Spouse	Adline Broadaway
Inferred Children	Walter Broadaway; Jo Broadaway

household members

Name	Age
Hary Broadaway	29
Adline Broadaway	25
Walter Broadaway	6
John Broadaway	4
Luvina Broadaway	2

KENNETH CRAIG BROADAWAY FAMILY
NORMA, PAMELA, PRISCILLA, BONNIE, TONYA, RODERICK BROADAWAY

family
is a gift that lasts
forever

BROADWAY & BROADAWAY COUSINS
Jerome, Marie, Jerome, Rod, Tonya; Cousins met in North Carolina.

family
is a gift that lasts
forever

RODRICK BROADAWAY ANCESTOR FAN TREE

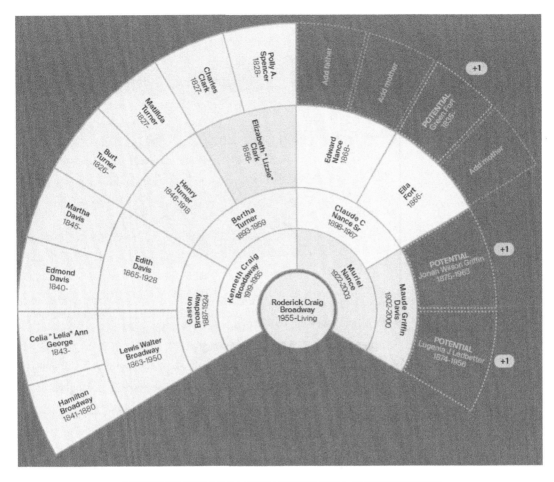

RODERICK BROADAWAY'S HORIZONTAL ANCESTRY TREE
GREAT GRANDFATHER HENRY TURNER 1846-1918 pictured below:

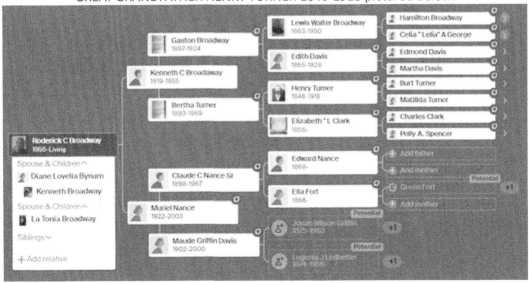

JAMES BAUCUM BROADAWAY (1820–1881)

James Broadaway is listed as a father on the marriage certificates of sons Marshall 1873, Calvin 1871

Spouses/Partners and children

Friend
- Charlotte Morris 1819–
- Marshall Baucum Broadaway 1850–1926

Spouse
- Harriet Miney Broadaway 1815–1885
- Calvin Broadaway 1840–1908

Friend
- Margaret Broadaway 1840–
- Jane Broadaway 1854–
- Mack Broadaway 1859–

The State of North Carolina,

No

_____ COUNTY.

To any ordained Minister of any Religious Denomination, or to any Justice of the Peace, for said county. _____ having applied to me for a license for the marriage of *Marshall Baucom* of *Lanesboro* aged 22 years, color *col* son of *Jas Broadway* and *Charlotte Morris* and _is living_ _is dead_ and reside at *Lanesboro* in the State of and *Silvy Clark* aged 16 years, color *col* daughter of *Saml Ingram* and *Hannah Clark* and _is living_ _is living_ and reside at _____ in the State of _____

And the written consent of _____ having been filed with me, and there being no legal impediment to such Marriage known to me, you are

Rites of Matrimony,

between *Calvin Broadaway* son of *Jim Broadway* and *Harriet Broadway* and *Anna Sturdivant* daughter of *Sia Sturdivant* and *Eliza Sturdivant* all of said County, and join them together as **Man** and **Wife.**

WITNESS, *John Stacy* Register of Deeds for said county, at Office in *Wadesboro* this 29 day of *Decr* in the ninety 6 year of American independence A. D. 1871. *John Stacy* R. D.

N2 State of North Carolina, *Anson* COUNTY.

To any Ordained Minister of any Religious Denomination, or to any Justice of the Peace for *Anson* County *William J. Moon* having applied to me for a License for the marriage of .... *Mack Broadaway* of *Anson* County, aged 22 years, color *Colored* son of *Jim Broadaway* and *Margaret Broadaway* and of whom *Jim Broadaway is dead* & *Margaret Broadaway is living*, and resides in *Anson* county, and State of North Carolina, †And *Viney Teal* of *Anson* county, aged 23 years, color *Colored* daughter of *Father's name not known* and *her mother's name is Viney Teal* and ~~of whom~~ *is living* and resides in the county and State aforesaid.

JAMES BAUCUM BROADAWAY buried - Old Westview Cemetery, Wadesboro, Anson North Carolina

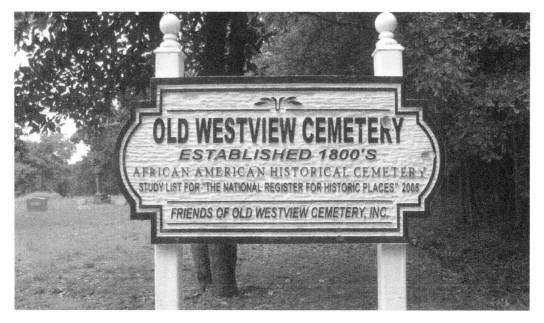

HARRIETT MINEY BROADAWAY

Slave Sale - January 4, 1836
Anson County NC Deed Book Z page 357

Frederick Staton To John Broadaway & wife.

Received of John Broadaway Jr. and Harriett Broadaway his wife Five hundred & fifty dollars in full payment of a Negro woman by the name of Miny about thirty one years of age for which Negro I warrant and forever defend the right and title from any other claims. I further relinquish my self & assigns etc. Jan. 4th 1836.

Test. Uriah Staton.   Frederick Staton (Seal)

March Term 1837. Then this Bill of sale was duly proven in open court by Uriah & ordered to be Registered.   W. D. Rogers Clk.

family
is a gift that lasts
—forever—

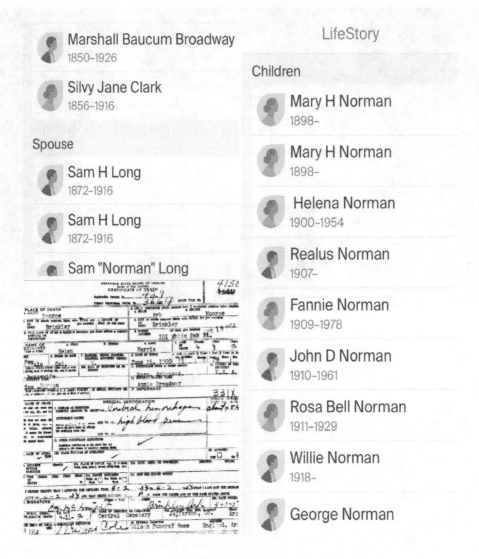

Marshall Baucum Broadway
1850–1926

Silvy Jane Clark
1856–1916

LifeStory

Spouse

Sam H Long
1872–1916

Sam H Long
1872–1916

Sam "Norman" Long

Children

Mary H Norman
1898–

Mary H Norman
1898–

Helena Norman
1900–1954

Realus Norman
1907–

Fannie Norman
1909–1978

John D Norman
1910–1961

Rosa Bell Norman
1911–1929

Willie Norman
1918–

George Norman

family
is a gift that lasts
forever

Robert 'Bob' Broadaway, Sidney Randall Broadaway, Amos James Broadaway, Francina Broadaway, and Anthony Broadaway

MARSHALL B. BROADWAY Family
Marshall B. and Silvia Clark Broadaway

NOT PICTURED
OLIVER
MARY F.
ANNIE L.
WILLIAM CANNIE
MARY E.

JOHN

MORRIS

LESSIE

SENIOR

JULIIS

SYLVIA CLARK BROADWAY and four cousins who are descendants of Marshall.
Eugene Broadway, Marie Broadway Toms, Jewel Broadway Farley, Jerome Turner

family
is a gift that lasts
forever

Child: Marie E. Br born in Marianna, AR 1917-1996
Last Child: Bernice (Lonnie) Br born in Flint, MI 1925-1995

BROADAWAY - MERRIWEATHER

OLIVER JAMES BROADAWAY 1874-1900

CHILDREN OF
OLIVER AND DORA BROADWAY

SAM   JOE   GREEN

MARSHALL'S   **NATHANIEL**   **CYNTHIA**
DAUGHTER
MARGARET

SAMUEL BROADWAY

DANIEL

GERALDINE

NAZAREE HANSBERRY
BROADWAY

SAM BROADWAY

LENNER   BOBBIE LEE   FLEECY

MINNIE MILLER BROADWAY

SAMELLA   VONITHA   FANNIE

DANIEL SR.

LEE ESTHER

GERRI

BOBBY

DANIEL
WITH 1ST COUSIN, HULAR SHACKLEFORD

DANIEL JR.

EUGENE

BOBBY

SKIP

DANIEL SR.

DANIEL SR.

DANIEL SR.

PEARL J. SMITH BROADWAY

CAROL

DANNY

NAZAREE

EUGENE

DANA

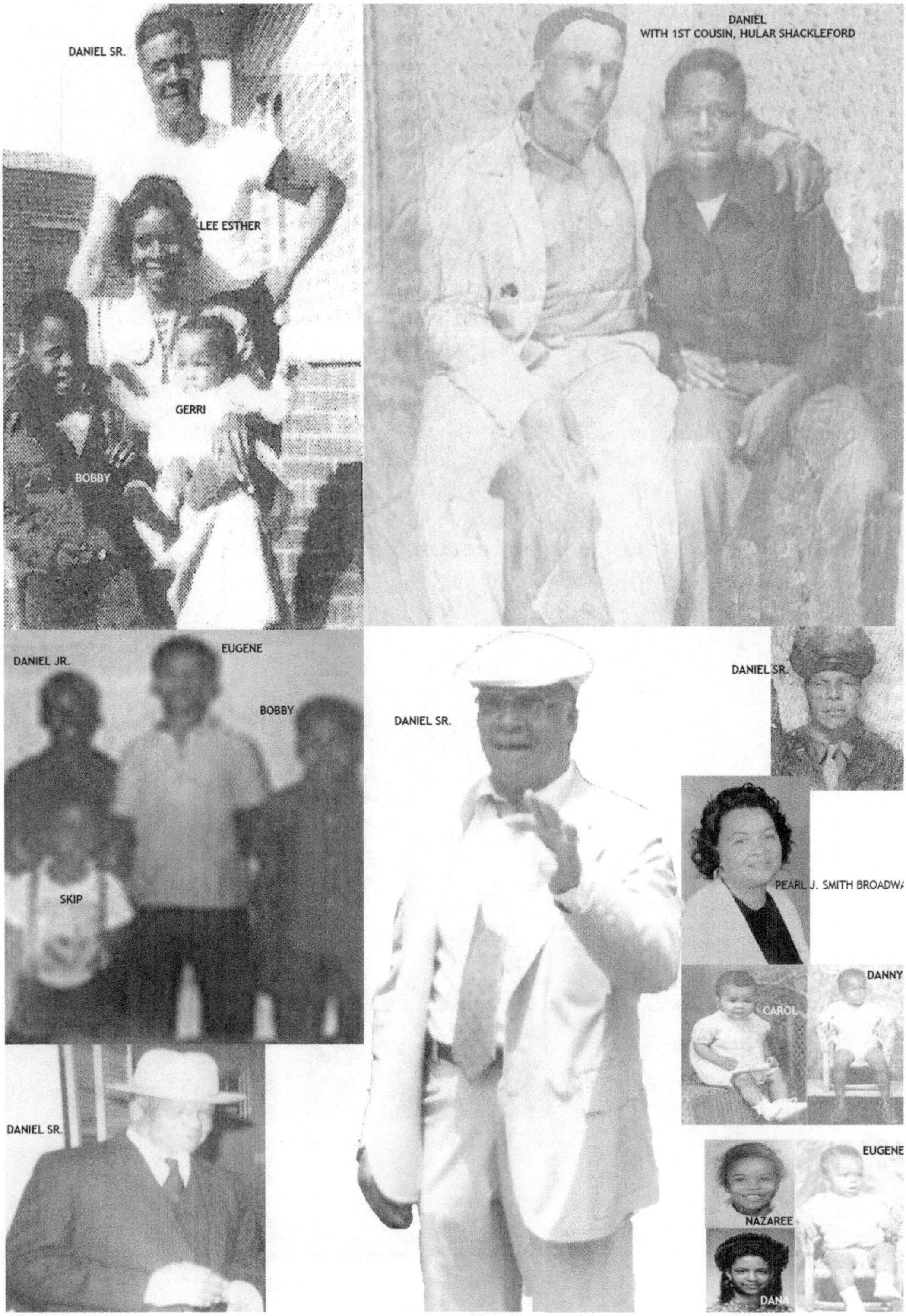

JOHN & LEE ETTA HANSBERRY
GREAT - GRANDPARENTS

HAZEL - LEE ETTA HANSBERRY
DAUGHTER & MOTHER

SAMUEL & GERALDINE BROADWAY
FATHER & DAUGHTER

JAMES &
PAULINE

BROADWAY-PARKER FAMILY

JONATHAN

HAZEL

MABEL

FELIX JR.

PARKER GUYS 1N 1965

CURTIS PARKER FAMILY

LENNER BROADWAY FAMILY

Lenner Broadway Sr.

Son:
Robert Broadway

Daughters:
Oneadia Broadway Kates
Marie Broadway Toms

Wife:
Parlee Peppers Broadway

Daughters:
Cecelia Broadway Tasby
Marilyn Broadway Worsham
Earma Broadway Brown

Son:
Lenner Broadway Jr.

Daughters:
Linda Broadway Howard
Minnie Lou Broadway

Son:
Renfort Bernard Broadway

Samella Broadway McKenzie

family
is a gift that lasts
forever

family
is a gift that lasts
forever

JOE BROADWAY FAMILY

JOE BROADWAY

AILEEN MARIE · AUDREY NITA · JOELLA

FREDDIE

JOE · ALFREDA

NITA

JOELLA

JOE JAKE · LINDA

MARIE

JOELLA WASHINGTON · DEBRA BROADWAY

JOELLA BROADWAY

GERALD · MANUEL AUNTJOELLA

family
is a gift that lasts
forever

GREEN JOE BROADWAY FAMILY

Roxanne Rosario

122

MARSHALL BROADWAY (son of Oliver Broadway)
(Marshall died before his daughter, Margaret was born),

NATHANIEL

NATHANIEL BROADWAY

NATHANIEL CYNTHIA EDDIE JESSIE WEST FAMILY

GREENE BROADWAY   ODELL BROADWAY   GREENE BROADWAY

GREENE & SAMUEL BROADWAY   JOE, SAM, & GREENE BROADWAY

CYNTHIA BROADWAY BURNETT

EDDIE BURNETT

JESSIE   WILLIE MAE   JAMMIE   BETTYE   EDNA

CYNTHIA BROADWAY

MARY ANN

ANNIE MAE
BURNETT
1929-1930

NOT PICTURED

ROSIE MAE

DORETHA

MARION

MARICE

ODELL

SAMUEL

JESSIE MAE

WILLIE MAE

JAMES

EDNA

BETTYE

JAMMIE

ARDELL

JOHN

124

family
is a gift that lasts
forever

family
is a gift that lasts
forever

family
is a gift that lasts
forever

family
is a gift that lasts
forever

MORRIS BROADWAY FAMILY

WILLIAM CANNIE BROADWAY'S FAMILY

family
is a gift that lasts
forever

LESSIE BROADWAY BEASLEY FAMILY

LESSIE BROADWAY
BEASLEY WILSON

CLIFTON BEASLEY

REV. ERNEST BEASLEY

ESTER BEASLEY

JAMES BEASLEY

ERMA BEASLEY

GEORGIA MAE BEASLEY

ELISHA BEASLEY

family
is a gift that lasts
forever

Robert "Bob" Broadway

Birth: 1817, Ansonville, Anson County, North Carolina
Death: 1881, Ansonville, Anson County, North Carolina

Family
Father: Cannis Broadway, 1795-1850
Mother: Female Broadway, 1795-

Spouse: Harriet "Minie" Broadway, 1810
Children:
1. Sidney R. Broadway, 1843-1923, (Spouse: Ella Jane Tyson 1862-1949)
2. Lydia Broadway, 1849- (child: Ellen Broadway 1866-)
3. Harriett Broadway 1855-

Spouse: Meallie Gould, 1835-
Children:
1. None

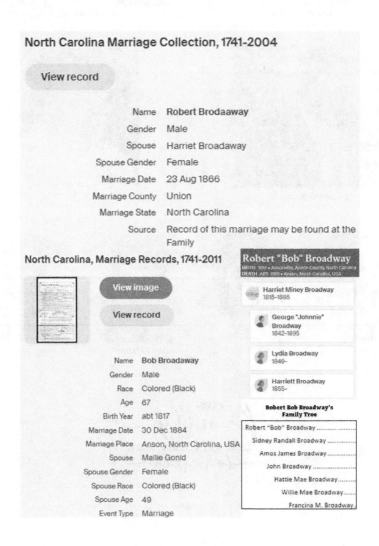

North Carolina Marriage Collection, 1741-2004

View record

Name	Robert Brodaaway
Gender	Male
Spouse	Harriet Broadaway
Spouse Gender	Female
Marriage Date	23 Aug 1866
Marriage County	Union
Marriage State	North Carolina
Source	Record of this marriage may be found at the Family

North Carolina, Marriage Records, 1741-2011

View image

View record

Name	Bob Broadaway
Gender	Male
Race	Colored (Black)
Age	67
Birth Year	abt 1817
Marriage Date	30 Dec 1884
Marriage Place	Anson, North Carolina, USA
Spouse	Mallie Gonld
Spouse Gender	Female
Spouse Race	Colored (Black)
Spouse Age	49
Event Type	Marriage

Robert "Bob" Broadway
BIRTH: 1817 • Ansonville, Anson County, North Carolina
DEATH: ABT. 1881 • Anson, North Carolina, USA

- Harriet Miney Broadway 1815-1885
- George "Johnnie" Broadway 1842-1895
- Lydia Broadway 1849-
- Harriett Broadway 1855-

Robert Bob Broadway's Family Tree

Robert "Bob" Broadway ....
Sidney Randall Broadway ....
Amos James Broadway ....
John Broadway ....
Hattie Mae Broadway ....
Willie Mae Broadway ....
Francina M. Broadway ....

Slave Sale – January 4, 1836
Anson County NC Deed Book Z page 357

Frederick Staton To John Broadaway &c urge.

Received of John Broadaway Jr. and Harriett Broadaway his wife Five hundred & fifty dollars in full payment of a Negro woman by the name of Miny about thirty one years of age for which Negro I warrant and forever defend the right and title from all claims whatever. I further relinquish myself & assigns &c. Jan. 4th, 1836.

Test. Uriah Staton.   Frederick Staton (seal)

Anson Jan. Sesc. 1837. Thus this Bill of sale was duly proven in open court by Uriah &
ordered to be Registered.   N. D. Boggan Clk.

SYDNEY BROADAWAY

State of North Carolina, Office Register of Deeds.
Anson County.   July 9   1887

To any Ordained Minister of any Religious Denomination, or to any
Justice of the Peace for Anson County:

Sidney Broadaway (colored) having applied to me for a license for
the marriage of himself, he being a Citizen of Anson County, aged 42 years,
color Colored, the son of Daniel Binton   and Minny Broadaway
the father now aged, the mother both, resident dead
And Ellen Tyson   of Anson County, aged 22 years,
color Colored, daughter of Charles Tyson   and Louisa Tyson
the father and, the mother both, resident of Anson County

family
is a gift that lasts
forever

Slave Sale – January 4, 1836
Anson County NC Deed Book Z page 357

Frederick Staton To John Broadaway &c &c.

Received of John Broadaway Jr. and Harriett Broadaway his wife Five hundred & fifty dollars in full payment of a Negro woman by the name of [illegible] about thirty one years of age for which Negro I warrant and forever defend the right and title from all other claims. I further relinquish my right & [illegible] &c. Jan. 4th 1836.

Test. Uriah Staton.   Frederick Staton (Seal)

Anson Jan. Term 1837. Then this Bill of sale was duly proven in open court by Uriah [illegible]

Wm B Rodman Clk

FROM WHOM HIRED	NAME AND OCCUPATION	TIME EMPLOYED	RATE OF WAGES	AMOUNT FOR EACH SLAVE	Amount Received (Dolrs / Cents)	SIGNATURE
R. Crump	Alfred	Laborer			12 00	
J. Edwards	Pink	"			12 00	
Thos Little	Allen	"			12 00	Thos Little
Wm Bennett	Silas	"			12 00	
J Crady	Frank	"			12 00	
Wm Allen	Ned	"			12 00	
Wm Sturtevant	Daniel	"			12 00	
J B Ingram	Mark	"			12 00	
B Ingram	Jim	"			12 00	
Jno Broadaway	Sidney	"			12 00	

September 6th 1857 Bap,

Upheld Isaac Davis, David Gaddy by Letter

Calvin Davis, Julious Carpenter by Letter

Dismissed James Barber, John M Thomas by Letter

Jesse Fifer

Sidney the property of Jno Broadaway

Returned to the Association at Piney Grove 1857

family
is a gift that lasts
forever

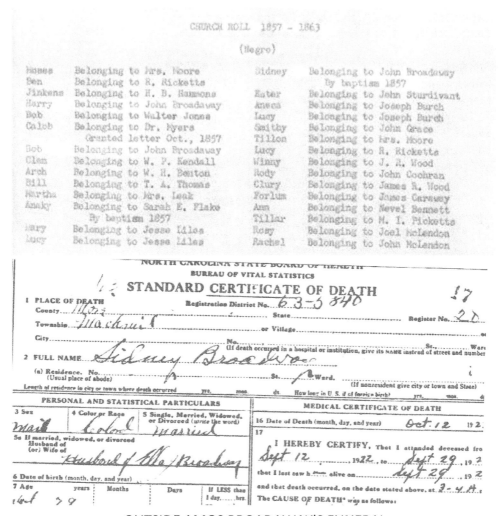

OUTSIDE AMOS BROADAWAY'S FUNERAL

Sidney Randall Broadway

Birth: 1843, Polkton, Anson County, North Carolina
Death: October 12, 1923, Moore, North Carolina

Family
Father: Daniel L. Benton, 1805-1893
Mother: Harriet "Minie" Broadway, 1810-

Spouse: Ella Jane Tyson, 1862-1949
Children:
1. Emma Tyson, 1881-
2. Sidney Randall Broadway Jr., 1889-1928, (Spouse: Pearl Eugene Curry 1897-1966; Children: Tona Broadway 1917-, Harley Broadway 1918-1994, Walter Lester Broadway 1928-1997; Spouse: Frances E. Williams 1890-; Children: Georgie Mae Broadway 1913-1994)
3. Amos James Broadway, 1893-1940
4. Gracie E. Broadway, 1895-1924 (Spouse: Simon Lowery 1903-1971; Child: Julius C. Lowery 1929-2003)
5. Charles Forester Broadway, 1898-1983 (Spouse: Amelia Jane Broadway 1899-1988)
6. Ellwood Broadway, 1902-1936 (Child: Gracie Broadway 1925-)
7. Oscar W. Broadway, 1907-1954 (Spouse: Aldonia McCullough 1909-)

Spouse: Cora Elizabeth Little, 1847-
Children:
1. Susan County, 1864- (Spouse: Joseph Threadgill Jr. 1862-; Child: Susan County 1864)
2. John Broadway, 1867-1946 (Spouse: Ann Eliza (Puss) Davis 1873-
3. Monroe Broadway, 1871-1947(Spouse: Martha Jane Deberry 1878-1941; Children: Howard Monroe Broadway 1910-1972, Edward Stelly Broadway 1914-1961, John Quincey Broadway 1916-1991, Nathaniel Lois Broadway 1918-1983)
4. Canny Broadway, 1873-1936 (Spouse: Cannie Geen 1889-)
5. Cora Anna Broadway, 1883-1933 (Spouse: George Steele 1863-1960; Children: James Steele 1906-, George H. Steele 1909-, Cora Evelyn Steele 1917-1996)

family
is a gift that lasts
forever

HARRIETT MINEY BROADAWAY, SLAVE

Harriet Miney Broadway 1815–1885
BIRTH ABT. 1815 • Ansonville Township, Anson County, North Carolina

Friend
Robert "Bob" Broadway 1817–1881
Children
George "Johnnie" Broadway 1842–1895
Lydia Broadway 1849–
Harriett Broadway 1855–

Spouse
James Baucum Broadway 1820–1881
Child: Calvin Broadway 1840–1908

Friend
Daniel L Benton 1804–1893
Child: Sidney Benton Broadway 1835–1923

Slave sale – January 4, 1836
Anson County NC Deed Book Z page 357

Frederick Staton to John Broadaway & wife.

Received of John Broadaway Jr. and Harriett Broadaway his wife Five hundred & fifty dollars in full payment of a Negro woman by the name of Miney about thirty one years of age for which Negro I warrant and forever defend the right and title from all other claims. I further relinquish myself & resign &c. Jan. 4, 1836.

Test. Uriah Staton.

Frederick Staton (Seal).

(Seal) Jan. Term 1837. Then this Bill of sale was duly proven in open court by Uriah & ordered to be Registered.

W. D. Rogers Clk.

family
is a gift that lasts
forever

George Broadway
1835-

Spouse & Children ∧

 Harriet Broadway

 Jenia Broadway

 Bose Broadway

 James E Broadway

 Dave Broadway

 Watt Broadway

 Charlotte C. Broadway

Spouse & Children ∧

 Phylis Parker

 George Wesly Maske

George Wesly Mask
Birth: March 1859, Ansonville, Anson County, North Carolina
Death: May 9, 1928, Hamlet, Richmond, North Carolina

Family
Father: George Broadway, 1795-1850
Mother: Phylis Parker

Spouse: Mary Thomas, 1861-
Children:
1. John Mass 1883-
2. Lonnie Mass 1884-1927
3. Joseph Mass 1885-
4. Hattie Mass 1887-
5. Miles Mass 1889-
6. Thomas Mass 1890-
7. John "Bunk" Mass 1893-1917
8. Henry Mass 1895-
9. Bertha Mass 1897-
10. George Viola Mass 1899-
11. Viola Mass 1900-
12. Mina Mass 1902-
13. Dora Mass 1904-1972
14. Janie Mass 1906-
15. Ed Mass 1908-

Spouse: Octavio Carter 1879-
Children: None listed

GEORGE BROADWAY

Name	George Broadaway
Age in 1870	35
Birth Date	abt 1835
Birthplace	North Carolina
Dwelling Number	274
Home in 1870	Lanesboro, Anson, North Carolina
Race	Black
Gender	Male
Post Office	Wadesboro
Occupation	Farm Laborer
Cannot Read	Yes
Cannot Write	Yes
Male Citizen Over 21	Yes
Inferred Spouse	Harriet Broadway

Household members

Name	Age
George Broadaway	35
Harriet Broadaway	

1870 Neighbor: Sidney 35 n Elizabeth 20 Broadway n child

1880 Neighbor: Harry 65 & Eliza 54 Broadway & children

1840-1883
Slaves during1863, Sidney n George Broadway were on Confederate Army
Payrolls for Enslaved Labor for John Broadway, Received $12 per/mo.

Name	George Broadaway
Age	46
Birth Date	Abt 1834
Birthplace	North Carolina
Home in 1880	Ansonville, Anson, North Carolina
Dwelling Number	101
Race	Black
Gender	Male
Relation to Head of House	Self (Head)
Marital Status	Married
Spouse's Name	Harlett Broadaway
Father's Birthplace	North Carolina
Mother's Birthplace	North Carolina
Occupation	Farmer
Cannot Read	Y
Cannot Write	Y
Neighbors	View others on page

Household members

Name	Age
George Broadaway	46
Hariett Broadaway	32
Jenia Broadaway	12
Bose Broadaway	9
Jim Broadaway	6
Watt Broadaway	2
Charlotte C. Broadaway	5/12

AUTHOR EUGENE BROADWAY – INSPIRED BY AFRICA'S RESEARCH

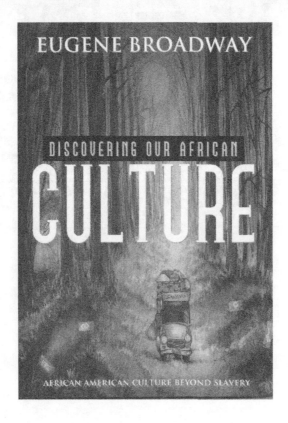

Toms
Family

2 — The Courier Index, Thursday, October 14, 2010

Broadway family   Submitted Photo

Several members of the Broadway Family of Marianna recently traveled to Chicago for a family reunion. During the reunion, family members reviewed a book on family history.

The Courier Index, Thursday, December 2, 2010 – 3

Book written by Moro native on Broadway family history donated to LC Public Library

Former Moro resident Marie Broadway Toms recently donated a copy of her genealogy book "Broadway Generations" to the Lee County Public Library.

The book was given to the library by Toms' mother, Parlee Broadway.

The book traces the family's historical beginnings in Anson County, North Carolina to James Broadway, a slave. In search of a better life, James' son, Marshall, later completed the six-month, wagon train journey from North Carolina to the rich, Delta farmland of Lee County, Arkansas in 1885. Marshall and Silvia Clark Broadway are Toms' great-great grandparents. Additionally, Oliver and Dora Reese Broadway are great-grandparents, Sam and Minnie Miller Broadway are grandparents and Lenner and Parlee Peppers Broadway are Toms' parents.

Toms released the Broadway book about the family, as promised, at the Broadway family reunion

Book donation   Photo by Rita Hirons

Parlee Broadway, right, on the behalf of her daughter Marie Toms, donates a copy of Toms' book, "Broadway Generations" to the Lee County Library. Betsy Bowman, left, accepts the book.

during July 2010 in Chicago. Not only was the book presented, but other former and current Lee County residents contributed in the event.

Jerome Turner of Chicago showcased the Broadway Family Picture booklet. Ken Broadway, of Little Rock, presented the oldest picture of Marshall and Silvia Broadway. Additionally, Eugene Broadway of Atlanta, Ga., marveled the group by gathering over 2,500 kinfolks on the Broadway Family Tree and placing them on MyHeritage.com and Ancestry.com websites. In addition, Earma Broadway-Brown of Dallas, an author and publisher of several books, started a Facebook campaign to find many of the relatives, performed research and built a web page for Marie Toms (www.marietoms.net) to inform family members about the reunion. Dr. Jonathan McKenzie, of Chicago, coordinated the efforts of the program booklet. Danny Broadway, of Memphis, painted a professional artwork that was used on the book cover and as the Broadway family reunion logo.

"Many more talented

family members were involved," said Parlee Broadway. "They also submitted stories and family tree information. One of the largest families who participated in this activity was Cynthia Broadway Burnett's family of 16 children.

"We were so happy when we stumbled upon the grave and marking of Silvia Broadway in a Springfield grave yard," Toms said. "We could see what care had been placed in getting her head stone."

Through the family committee's research, a picture of Marshall and Silvia Broadway was discovered. "For an African-American family, a picture from the late 1800s or early 1900s is a wonderful find," Toms continued. "We Broadways can all celebrate our heritage of African-American and Cherokee Indian."

"Historically the book is written about Broadway legacy, but all who read would agree that the book is for anyone desiring to learn about their families, promoting family values, legacies, family tree research and writing their own book," Toms said.

family
is a gift that lasts
forever

Book donated   *Photo by Katie West*

Parlee Broadway donates a copy of the book "The Journey" to the Lee County/Marianna Library on behalf of her nephew and the book's author, Eugene Broadway. The book is the third in a series of genealogy books about the Broadway family. Parlee has donated a copy of all three books to the library.

The Journey by Eugene Broadway

ANSON COUNTY NORTH CAROLINA RESEARCH TEAM

family is a gift that lasts forever

AFRICAN RESEARCH TEAMS (Pictured Above)

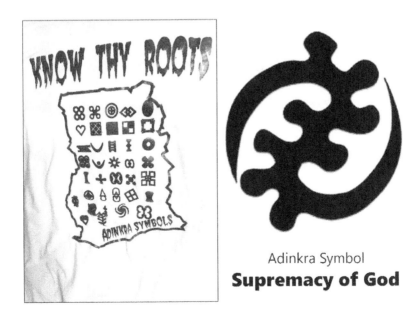

Adinkra Symbol
Supremacy of God

AFRICAN RESEARCH TEAMS

AFRICAN RESEARCH TEAMS (Pictured Above and Below)

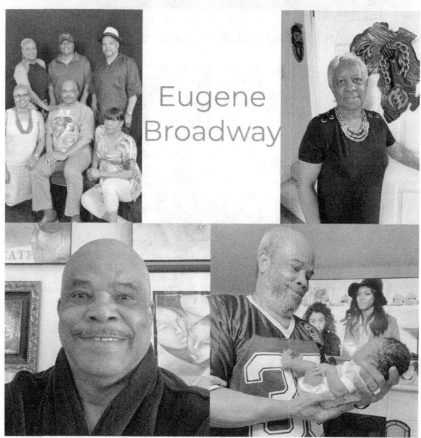

Eugene Broadway

MARIE BROADWAY TOMS FAMILY (ABOVE AND BELOW)

MARIE BROADWAY TOMS FAMILY (ABOVE AND BELOW)

JEROME TURNER FAMILY (Son of Fleecy Mae Broadway Turner)

family
is a gift that lasts
forever

Jerome Turner Family (Son of Fleecy Mae Broadway Turner)

family
is a gift that lasts
forever

END NOTES

Ancestry Sources for all the family members featured in this book

- 1800 United States Federal Census
- 1810 United States Federal Census
- 1820 United States Federal Census
- 1830 United States Federal Census
- 1840 United States Federal Census
- 1850 U.S. Federal Census - Slave Schedules
- 1850 United States Federal Census
- 1860 U.S. Federal Census - Slave Schedules
- 1860 United States Federal Census
- 1870 United States Federal Census
- 1880 United States Federal Census
- 1900 United States Federal Census
- 1910 United States Federal Census
- 1920 United States Federal Census
- 1930 United States Federal Census
- 1940 United States Federal Census (Beta)
- 1950 United States Federal Census
- Added by confirming a Smart Match
- Almaree Broadway
- American Civil War Soldiers
- Ancestry Family Trees
- Ancestry sources
- Arkansas, Birth Certificates, 1914-1917
- Arkansas, County Marriages Index, 1837-1957
- Arkansas, Death Certificates, 1914-1969
- Arkansas, Marriage Certificates, 1917-1969
- Beta: Newspapers.com Obituary Index, 1940-1955
- Branson's North Carolina business directory: containing facts, figures, names, and locations, revised, and corrected annually.
- Citation information
- Confederate Applications for Presidential Pardons, 1865-1867
- Cook County, Illinois Death Index, 1908-1988
- Delaware, U.S., Death Records, 1861-1933
- Event: Smart Matching Role: 8001181
- Family Data Collection - Births
- Family Data Collection - Individual Records
- Geneanet Community Trees Index

- Global, Find A Grave Index for Non-Burials, Burials at Sea, and other Select Burial Locations, 1300s-Current
- Illinois, Deaths, and Stillbirths Index, 1916-1947
- Indiana, Death Certificates, 1899-2011
- Millennium File
- Muster rolls of the soldiers of the War of 1812: detached from the Militia of North Carolina in 1812 and 1814
- New York, New York, U.S., Index to Death Certificates, 1862-1948
- North Carolina Birth Index, 1800-2000
- North Carolina Census, 1790-1890
- North Carolina Death Certificates, 1909-1975
- North Carolina Death Collection, 1908-2004
- North Carolina Marriage Bonds, 1741-1868
- North Carolina Marriage Collection, 1741-2004
- North Carolina Wills
- North Carolina, Deaths, 1906-1930
- North Carolina, Land Grant Files, 1693-1960
- North Carolina, Marriage Records, 1741-2011
- North Carolina, U.S., Death Certificates, 1909-1976
- North Carolina, U.S., Land Grant Files, 1693-1960
- North Carolina, U.S., Marriage Records, 1741-2011
- North Carolina, U.S., Newspapers.com™ Stories and Events Index, 1800s-current
- North Carolina, U.S., Wills and Probate Records, 1665-1998
- North Carolina, Wills and Probate Records, 1665-1998
- Ohio, County Marriages, 1774-1993
- Other information
- Search on Ancestry
- Social Security Death Index
- South Carolina, Chesterfield County, Original Marriage licenses, 1911-1951
- Tennessee, Death Records, 1908-1958
- Transcript
- U.S. City Directories (Beta)
- U.S. City Directories, 1821-1989 (Beta)
- U.S. IRS Tax Assessment Lists, 1862-1918
- U.S. Phone and Address Directories, 1993-2002
- U.S. Public Records Index, Volume 1
- U.S. World War II Draft Registration Cards, 1942
- U.S. WWII Draft Cards Young Men, 1898-1929
- U.S., Confederate Army Payrolls for Enslaved Labor, 1840-1883
- U.S., Find A Grave Index, 1600s-Current
- U.S., Find A Grave Index, 1700s-Current
- U.S., Find a Grave® Index, 1600s-Current
- U.S., Index to Public Records, 1994-2019

- U.S., Pardons Under Amnesty Proclamations, 1865-1869
- U.S., Social Security Applications and Claims Index, 1936-2007
- U.S., World War I Draft Registration Cards, 1917-1918
- Unsourced Citation
- Unsourced Citation
- War of 1812 Service Records
- Web: North Carolina, Find A Grave Index, 1716-2012
- Web: North Carolina, Find A Grave Index, 1729-2011
- World War I Draft Registration Cards, 1917-1918
- History.com
- Defining Freedom | National Museum of African American History and ...
- si.edu https://nmaahc.si.edu › exhibitions › reconstruction › def...
- History & Culture - Reconstruction Era National Historical Park (U.S. ...
- nps.gov https://www.nps.gov
- African American Homesteaders in the Great Plains - National Park Service
- nps.gov https://www.nps.gov › articles › african-american-homest...
- https://www.history.com/news/reconstruction-timeline-steps

family
is a gift that lasts
forever

ABOUT THE AUTHOR

Marie Toms, 45-year educator, author, technology college instructor, and serial business owner latest contribution to the Family Heritage Collection of books is 'The Broadaway Slave Journey introducing newly discovered branch of Broadaway family.

Mrs. Toms says her success work ethics came from humble beginnings on the family farm where her work along with other siblings included chopping and picking cotton, driving tractors to plow the land, cooking breakfast for the family, cleaning and performing various chores. Additionally, working in the church, attending and teaching Sunday School students enhanced her values.

As a high school educator, she taught Business Education at Francis Howell High School in St. Charles County of Missouri. Later She served as their Business Department Coordinator for ten-plus years. Before retiring, Mrs. Toms served as the A+ School Grant Writer and implemented the A+ Schools Free College Tuition Program for their high school students for five years.

Her recognition as a high school educator includes Teacher of the Year, various Missouri district awards, St. Charles Community Award, Missouri A+ Schools Advisory Board, Conference Speaker, and National Business Education Conference Facilitator.

Upon retiring, Mrs. Toms started another career as a Business and Technology instructor at The Stevens Institute of Business and Arts College (SIBA) for nineteen years.

In her spare time, she has owned multiple direct marketing businesses, plus researching, and writing genealogy books, photo story books, and a life insurance producer.

Mrs. Toms currently lives in St. Louis, Missouri with her husband Leonard. They are empty nesters with two grown sons, Leonard, Jr, with a career in the Airbnb industry and Kilian, is a European Executive for a Fortune 500 company. As a retired educator, she enjoys family research, travelling and cooking.

OTHER BROADWAY BOOKS

Broadway Books Available with Author

- Broadway Generations – Marie Toms

- The Journey – Eugene Broadway

- Broadway Connections – Dennis J. Turner

- Broadway Royals – Eugene Broadway, Marie Toms, Jerome Turner

- Discovering Your African Culture – Eugene Broadway.

GETTING STARTED WITH FAMILY RESEARCH

Where does one start with family history and research. I've discovered the best thing to start with is a desire to know your family. As a teenager around sixteen, it dawned on me that I hardly knew any of my huge family at that time. I said to myself I could be born in this area, live, go to school, graduate, work at a local bank, drive by these houses and neighborhoods and never really know anyone with the last name Broadway. I was talking to my mom, Parlee Peppers-Broadway and she said, why don't we change that? You should know family.

So, we started the journey together. Mom and I went from family to family and house to house. I met Broadway cousins, uncles, friends, aunts I would have never known. We took pictures. I interviewed elder family members, wrote stories and their life's whys. I ended up with quite a collection.

That was then. I wish I could say I kept the notes, pictures, and stories. For a long time, I did. Flash forward to the now season, I was talking to a family member about their desire to do family history research and a collaboration was born. It turned out several family members shared this desire to see family history explored and recorded. Maybe, your family does too. So, what are you waiting for? Get started soon – just by talking to family members to see who shares your passion to see family history honored and recognized.

NOTES

Made in the USA
Middletown, DE
31 August 2024

60085138R00104